Y0-CBF-230

When Lilacs Bloom

Anne Scherer

FORTNER
BOOKWORKS

These stories and columns originally appeared in *The Senior Reporter* magazine, which has graciously given its permission to reprint them in this book.

© Copyright 1996 by Anne Scherer

Published by:
Fortner BookWorks
5302 Ramsey Street
Duluth, Minnesota 55807
(218) 624-4949
(800) 360-WORD

All rights reserved. Except for short excerpts for review purposes, no part of this book may be reproduced or transmitted in any form by any means—electronic or mechanical, from photocopier to cyberspace—without permission in writing from the publisher.

Printed in the state of Minnesota in the United States of America by Bang Printing.

10 9 8 7 6 5 4 3 2 1

Cover and book design by Kollath Graphic Design; Duluth, Minnesota

Library of Congress Cataloging in Publication Data
96-60600

ISBN 0-9645557-0-0

I dedicate this book to my mother,
Lenore Rose Ehrens Shenkin.
This is my gift,
as she always wanted
her name in print.

Acknowledgments

*I*n writing the acknowledgments for this book I would be remiss if I did not thank every person who put a finger to a keyboard or wielded pencil or pen to get this together. I do not know exactly who they all are, but they do, and I want them to know that I am grateful.

I am in awe of those people who juggle words to make them come to life with expression. These of course are those who edit, and *to* them I am thankful and *for* them I am thankful.

I can't go beyond this third paragraph without thanking Larry Fortner. He called one day, some years ago, and asked, "Do you want to write a column?" He never even said *try to write* a column. He had confidence in me right from the start, and so many times I have felt grateful for his respect.

Then there is my family. My husband, Alan, and my boys Gary and Joe. They have been exposed in print for all to know and judge. This exposure for the boys began back in their tender teenage years when privacy is preferred to being displayed on the pages of a magazine that is distributed to thousands of homes. They were always gracious, even if more than a little worried from month to month about the content of the next column.

I thank my extended family, too ... my sister, nieces, godson, cousins ... all have been touched by my pen.

And Mama. Her dream was to write. She wrote dozens of short stories, and they were rejected. She even took a writing course and at the time of her death was writing a manuscript by hand. It must have been from her that I get the ability to put feelings into words that touch our lives.

And to Steven, who died at the age of 19, I must acknowledge that his life and the need to keep his memory alive is always in my heart. It is, after all, due to him that for us we know a time When Lilacs Bloom.

Anne Scherer
Duluth, Minnesota

Introduction

Anne Scherer feigns disinterest in sports. That's guy stuff, she would have you believe. I have unimpeachable evidence, however, that her life has been virtually obsessed with sports. I have observed with my own eyes and ears this woman yelling attaboys —not always at boys. I have heard "nice pitch!" from this woman. I have heard "good shot!" I have seen her north country home in fast-frozen Duluth decorated in key-lime green and Orange Bowl orange in honor of the University of Miami's New Year's adventures on national television. Oh, she cares, all right. Everything in her life, in fact, gets nothing less than her full and unstinting attention.

Works hard. Plays hard. Loves hard. Hurts hard. Writes with depth and power that bring joy and sorrow and tears and laughter. Oh, she cares, all right.

Some years back, in one of the better moments of my career, I asked Anne to begin writing a column for my magazine, *The Senior Reporter*. The only time I regret that decision is when people tell me that the first thing they look for in *The Reporter* is Anne's column. (Not *mine!*)

As further proof of my wisdom, I am proud and delighted to present this compilation of Anne's columns (not mine) to you in *When Lilacs Bloom*.

Good reading,

Larry Fortner

Editor and Publisher
The Senior Reporter / Fortner BookWorks
Duluth, Minnesota

Stories

Stories

≿♠

Musings

Killer B's

As a young married, when I imagined my life with Alan, I dreamed of all the stages we might go through together.

As it turned out, we didn't have much of a carefree, newly married stage because just a few weeks shy of our first anniversary we became parents.

Our years as young parents were hectic ones, with three boys and baseball and Scouts and PTA and music lessons and everything else that goes with that beehive existence.

As the boys got older they dropped some activities and added others, but Alan and I remained active in their lives. Currently, however, we are only somewhat involved. They are away from home, at school and at work. While we do help in their decision-making and manage to catch some of Joe's ballgames, basically Alan and I live alone.

I had imagined that at this stage of life we would have a lot of shared activity. In my dreams, Alan and I would picnic and stroll together. We would play cards and read on quiet evenings. Together we would take special-interest classes and go on weekend retreats. Joy would come from our togetherness.

While we *do* do some of these things, some of the time, the key phrase is: *In my dreams.*

When we are not involved in our separate activities and do spend evenings together, they follow a definite pattern: After dinner I clean the kitchen, and Alan retreats to his den to do some paperwork. I then sit in the living room rocker to watch TV and Alan migrates to the bedroom to watch TV.

Why do we not watch TV together? What came between us and my dreams?

What came between us and our life of shared time is an evil and consuming satanic device, one that rules the minds of men. It is the remote control.

I have no intention of beating this issue to death; innumerable articles already have been written about it. I write only because I have figured out the reasoning behind the obsessive actions of a man with a remote.

Women have spent an enormous amount of time wondering how a man can click fifty times in twenty seconds, hear hundreds of blips, see dozens of flashing images and from this sensory deluge decide which programs are bad and which are worth watching.

We (me being a part of the sisterhood of women) need a minute or more per click to determine the worth of a program. That is because we women are looking for content.

Men, on the other hand, are looking for one of the four B's. Yes, four B's.

They are balls, blood, bombs and bosoms. If any of these appear in a click, the man has hit paydirt. A problem develops when there are two or more men in a room if one is remote controlling and the other has different "B" priorities. Take my boys, for example.

Joe is a ball, bomb, blood, bosom guy while Gary is more your blood, ball, bomb, bosom type. This is explosive. Also, it results in sneaky ploys to gain remote control control. A guy thing.

So, you see, men don't really understand what they see during a fast-click sequence, such as this one:

"Ha"/click.

"Humph"/click.

"My"/click.

"Love"/click.

"Touchdowwwwnnnnnn!"

Pause.

They merely search for a "B" safety net.

I know that the women of the world are grateful for my insights and I wish them many years of rewarding TV viewing.

And to the men:

"Best wi-"/click.

Sorry—I know better.

Joe's Home
—Joe's Gone

I can't believe that a child, especially one who is no longer a child, could come home for summer and bring with him such havoc. I'm talking about our youngest, Joe.

First let's start with a daily routine—something you can count on and plan your day around. With Joe home again, I had to throw the concept of routine out the window. Some days began at eight-thirty in the morning. Other days began after noon. It all depended on weather and tee-time availability.

Next there was laundry. I would go downstairs, look at the hamper area and size up three or four loads. Then with a simple, "Joe, you want to throw your dirty clothes down the chute?" I would unleash an avalanche and find myself downwind of eight loads of wash.

Then there was his room. All I could do in there was change linen. Anything else was too hazardous. The floor was strewn with clothes (whether clean or dirty, known only to him), unpacked boxes brought from school, various items of sports equipment and other young-man stuff ad infinitum.

I just took a stick and beat a path to the bed and out again.

I also must have straightened the bathroom ten times daily. How anyone approaching adulthood could be so oblivious to his devastation was beyond belief. After he had showered, I would enter the room and find the shower curtain all crunched up, two wet towels on the floor along with dirty clothes, shoes and a baseball cap. The sink would have whiskers in it and a brush on it, along with shaving cream and toothpaste.

The downstairs was Joe's sanctum. There he had his CD player, a color TV with cable and remote, his video game player and a rocker recliner. There was also a little end table that truly should have been in the Guinness Book of Records for most glasses piled upon. On our daily trek to Joe's world we would often retrieve three to ten glasses, depending on whether he had entertained.

The first round of phone calls would start at around eight a.m. and could stretch to eleven. Those were the ones regarding golf.

Then from six p.m. until nine-thirty there could be another dozen calls that all began, "Joe, whatcha doin'?" "Nothing, what's going on?" My guess was that they took the best three "what's going ons" and planned the evening.

I can't tell you how many times I wished for the phone to stop ringing or the bathroom to stay neat, which simply proves once again that you'd better be careful what you wish for.

Came a Saturday when Joe left to report to football camp at school in St. Paul. He packed all morning, had brunch with us and left.

I haven't cleaned his room yet, but it won't take long. It's very empty. Besides, there's no great rush, since it will stay clean for a long time. So will the bathroom and the downstairs. The laundry is back to normal proportions and the phone rings … well … let's just say it's all very normal.

Joe doesn't plan to come home for any more summers. I have to accept this as part of a pattern already established. His older brother, Gary, comes home only about six times a year.

So I have to take the summer's memory and stash it someplace special, because with all the mess and bother and inconvenience came something undeniably, richly satisfying: kids at the door constantly; comings and goings in a frenzy; cheering at ballgames; people chattering and laughing; discarding pizza boxes; emptying pop cans.

Neat and tidy, routine and quiet have their place, but I think they can be overrated. I know for a fact that an awful lot of life and energy packed up and left at one p.m. on the Saturday when Joe took off.

So much for some wishes.

Back to School

When I was a kid I dreaded Labor Day because it meant going back to school. Except for getting new clothes, there was nothing to recommend the beginning of a new academic year. Mind you, I was a good student and had lots of friends. But the regimentation, the five days a week and the eight-to-three stuff weren't my cup of tea.

Today, now that I'm all grown up, Labor Day and those days that follow represent a sense of normalcy … a returning to routine.

In a few days, we will load a van full of Gary's possessions and take him back to school at St. Thomas. Joe, my younger son, also will return to school, which means that every day he will leave early and not return home until some eleven and a half hours later, after football practice. My husband, too, will vacate the premises from at least eight in the morning to six in the evening. It's normal, and it works ... but, where does that leave me?

Well, let's go back to Gary's room. He's gone, but is the room empty? Not quite!

There are socks, shirts and jewelry. Each item absolutely must have been taken by someone else or left somewhere because, when he was packing, to quote him, "It's gone and someone had to take it because I left it right here on my dresser and I looked everywhere!"

I will now gather all these forever-missing items and mail them to him at an expense probably greater than their combined worth. I will take down posters and gather memorabilia so important at the time but now left behind. I will re-arrange the furniture so that there is a navigable path between door and closet.

But most exciting of all is seeing the rug again. That happens after we throw away fast-food containers and gum wrappers.

Then I will attack the dirty dishes. And glasses with totally unrecognizable stuff on the bottom.

I have soaked and scraped these for days before suddenly realizing I was savagely trying to save a plastic glass with a Smurf on it.

Yessir, with things back to normal, I can even be sure the bathroom door will open. Often, I can barely squeeze in because there are sneakers and sweat clothes dropped behind it.

It's great when the routine returns and I can wash towels once a week.

Which brings to mind some questions:

Why, if we dry a clean body, do we need two new towels for each shower? And why do all the hooks I put up go unused while the wet towels are in a lump on the floor?

Then there's the decorative little hand towel I hang up. It's just to look pretty — but it's always used. This scares me because I don't know what it's used *for*. So when I *don't* put one out, what else do they use for whatever they use it for?

Well … these are academic questions now, because we are back to normal.

Normalcy also will take care of the ice issue. My boys have always been told, "Don't use all the ice in a tray and not refill it!" There have been many summer days when ice was at a premium because the freezer contained four trays — each with one cube. The admonition, "Don't use all the ice," is too open-ended. Leave one cube in the tray and you're in the clear.

Now, don't say I didn't raise them right. I did

my best. I punished, and always tried to make the punishment fit the crime. This got harder as they began to drive. You can't hit every fast-food place and say, "Don't serve this child a cold drink. He doesn't refill ice trays."

Oh, there's more. When they're all home there's never milk. There is when I go to sleep, but when I'm making coffee and cereal some six hours later, it's gone. I'm left with a refrigerator that is full of empty containers that for some reason are being chilled.

Now that my home has returned to normal, the bedrooms, bathroom and kitchen will be havens with a place for everything and everything in its place. With no one home all day, the house will stay neat for sure. The phone will ring half as much and the doors won't slam with comings and goings and all the hubbub will settle down.

And the more I reflect on the tranquility, the more I realize that I still dread Labor Day, because it means going back to school.

Mama's Touch

I have discovered that while I may enjoy the social amenities of being a woman, in truth my spirit is fiercely independent. You may open a door for me as a gesture to my femininity, and it's marvelous; but open it because I'm incapacitated, and I hate it. Further, I have trouble asking for help.

But I could always be comfortable asking Mama. She epitomized comfort and care.

I miss Mama dearly.

I should explain why I am being so introspective. I fell and fractured my wrist a few weeks ago. Therefore, I have been dependent on my family for many things. And they really have tried to help.

There is a difference, however, between what they can do for me and what Mama would have done. I offer an example:

If I were confined to bed, my husband might give me lunch and turn on my TV. He'd see to it that the telephone was near me and that I had a drink. Then he would take off for an afternoon at the Y.

Mama, on the other hand, would take care of the same necessities, but she would also stroke my forehead, tie back my hair, watch a game show with me or chat for a while. No matter how sick I felt, I knew that I was not alone.

The boys were home recently, and, while my handicap didn't dampen the pleasures of the visit, it did require some extra help on their part. They are used to being asked to help with our animals, or to reach something, or to open something, but this holiday was definitely different. Their chores included peeling and chopping and slicing and dicing.

I mention this because one of my best memories of this otherwise unmemorable experience came when I asked my son Gary to help me button my coat. A look crossed his face that I read as annoyance or disdain. I immediately recoiled and buttoned up myself, although not correctly. I must admit that I felt deeply hurt.

The next day I forgot to get dressed before my husband left. As I puffed and umphed and struggled to put on something as personal as my bra, in walked Gary without a bit of hesitation to help me. I told him of my reaction to the previous incident and he said, "Oh no! I was unnerved that you needed help. It was unnatural, when you're always there for us." It was a moment I have put on a freeze frame to relive in my memory many times.

In the midst of this visit with its unnatural events, my son Joe became ill twice. First he spent three hellish days with the flu. He fought fevers of 104 degrees and survived horrendous accompanying symptoms. Upon recovery, he was up for three days but then was felled again for several more with a secondary infection.

Joe is not one to allow displays of showy affection, but he will tolerate a little attention.

During his flu battle, I set my alarm for every half hour during the night until his fever came down from the dangerously high level. I kept ginger ale at his bedside and a cool cloth on his head. When he dozed, I seized the chance to kiss his cheek or hold his hand. As he thrashed restlessly, I was in the rocker across from him to rearrange covers or engage in chatter. After his fever-breaking sweats, I was there with a dry shirt, a cool, clean pillowcase and freshening body powder. And I did the dance of joy for him when he was normal for twenty-four hours.

Why did I do all this? Well, it is the Mama in me. Not the natural maternal instinct, but the Lenore—*my* Mama—in me. She would have done no less.

Joe is back at school and well. There was no "Thank you." There didn't have to be. But, someday in the future, when he's ministering to his own child, I hope he remembers what it was like to never be alone.

Empty Chair

*I*t was the eve of Rosh Hashanah, the Jewish New Year. In my heart was the feeling of a holiday. In my oven, half a turkey breast and potatoes.

Wine and a round challah bread were ready. Fresh flowers were set near the apples drizzled with honey—traditional symbols of sweetness and continuity.

I put out the candles to light for the blessing and sat in the rocker while waiting for Alan.

As I rocked I thought of my sister in Miami.

As I rocked I thought of my cousins in Dallas. Wives and husbands and children would all be gathered to share the New Year.

My sister's table would include two daughters, a son-in-law, a grandson, husband and mother-in-law. The picture was warm, and good.

As I rocked I looked at my table festooned with linen and silver and china, bedecked with flowers and candles and steeped in tradition. But I saw only two places set and three empty chairs. I had wished Joe a Happy New Year on Saturday when I was at his school for his football game. I hoped that, as he grabbed a Big Mac that night, he had at least remembered the day.

I don't know if we have been given the right to life, liberty and the pursuit of self pity, but there I was, wallowing in it. That's all we ever do with self pity. We never swim in it, embrace it, visit it. We wallow in it.

The only value I see to this process is that sometimes some really deep thoughts surface when your heart is on the floor.

I began to think of the value of human life. I sat there missing my son Steven and my mother so much that I felt like an open wound with edges that would never meet and heal. The value of their lives to me, and to the many who knew them, is immeasurable.

In tragic contrast was a television show about gangs I recently watched. A young person of around seventeen said that, in essence, killing his first person was hard, but wasn't a problem after that.

On that same show I watched a "drive-by." That's when a group in a car drives by another group of young people and randomly shoots. They do not know if or whom they kill. The young man being interviewed said, "See, that's a drive-by," casually, as if he had just swatted a mosquito.

In a short period of time recently I saw stories about a man killing his family, putting them in a freezer for twelve years and beginning a new life and new family. I saw two young boys who had killed their abusive father. I saw yet another murder of a Miami vacationer. I saw an article complaining that the tourist murders were getting so much attention that the multitude of everyday murders went hardly noticed.

And, during the peace-treaty signing, I saw and heard Israeli Prime Minister Rabin say, "Enough is enough!" He referred to the killing and bloodshed and widows and orphans and parents burying their own. Finally, a great moment that makes us look forward with hope—but never to forget the number of people who died, many of them innocent bystanders, before terrorists and statesmen said, "Enough."

Why is murder so easy and the value of human life so cheap? Is it weakened church and family relationships? Has the hippie generation failed as parents?

Or is it plain and simple boredom, leading to trouble?

I don't pretend to know. Each theory could keep a social scientist busy for a year without necessarily solving or changing anything.

All I know is real people stuff, like a table set for just two and a heart on the floor and the pain of loss. And I reach out to every mother, widow and child who also hurts. We know the value of human life. We know so much more than the kid who can kill without remorse. We know the reality of an empty chair at a holiday table.

The Nose Knows

Why is it that I am the expert on all things that are "rotten in Denmark?" My family will remove a package of deli goodies from the refrigerator and suspect that it is spoiled. They will bring it to me and ask me to smell it. Why? "How does it smell to you?" I will ask. They will reply that it smells bad and appears slimy. Why, then, is a second opinion in order? If I say that the item in question is okay, would they be dumb enough to go ahead and eat something so revoltingly unappetizing? I confirm that it is slimy and smells like old sneakers. I congratulate them on their ability to sense these things and then remind them that one day they will have to make these momentous decisions on their own.

Cinderella

"You have to come," Roberta said. She was my good friend and also a fraternity hostess at the University of Miami. She was imploring me to attend a Thanksgiving party for the Pi Kappa Alphas who couldn't go home for the holiday.

"You know how I feel about fraternity men, Berta. They're so shallow."

"Well, keep your idealistic self intact and come for *me*," she said.

And so I went, and was the belle of the ball. The night created a Cinderella memory.

There was a group of young men seated together, and I had been approached by most of them. One, however, had looked but not spoken. He was dressed in white, had a crew cut, a cleft chin and sensual lips. When we were finally introduced, he smiled and displayed the two deepest dimples I had ever seen. His name was Alan, and he made my heart sing as we talked and danced the night away.

We were inseparable for the rest of the evening and have been together for the rest of our lives. That New Year's Eve he asked me to be his date for all New Year's Eves to come, and I agreed.

Now it is November and I am nestled between Gold and Silver. In October Alan was fifty, and this Christmas Day we will have been married for twenty-five years.

I was nineteen and he was twenty-five. I had met an older man, and it was exciting. He had been in the Army and in Ethiopia. I was going to look on a globe and see exactly where that was.

He wanted to join the Peace Corps, and so he had ideals. He was going to be an accountant, and so he had ambition. He had played the saxophone, and so he was many-faceted including, at least, music. He played sports, and so he was vital and virile. And on our first date we went to a Miami-Notre Dame football game. Miami was not a powerhouse then, but that night it held Notre Dame to a scoreless tie. I looked over at him, and the thrill of it all had brought tears to his eyes. He could cry! I was a goner!

Over the years he has gained a reputation of being absent-minded. This is very unfair. True, he has lost thousands of combs, dozens of wallets and scads of checkbooks, but so what? He *did* lose the car, but only once. And once he misplaced two of the three boys, but that's another story and, besides, a friend found them.

Does he have any bad points? Of course, but in truth they rarely surface, except for his "mad face," which he denies having and that everyone hates. At home he is a loving, gentle man who adores tranquility and fun.

One morning a few weeks ago, he turned to me and, although he only stroked my face, made passionate love. As a newer bride I would not have understood this kind of lovemaking. It takes a mellowed bride to feel passion from him saying, "My greatest desire in life is to grow old with you."

I cried, because I was looking into the eyes of a young man dressed in white, who makes my heart sing—a man who doesn't age. His hair has no gray (his beard is all gray). His face is a round little boy face (maybe there are jowls if you look). His hands have thrown basketballs, bowling balls and baseballs. They have suffered multiple athletic breaks, but I don't look when he tries to rub away a little arthritic pain now and again. He still has his jump shot and court presence when he plays basketball each week, although he has slowed down and has to favor his knees. Maybe I cry because when I look at me the mirror works both ways and I see myself aging, but time stands still when I look at him.

I have been adored by this man. I can be in a threadbare robe and told I am beautiful. I can be in a pit of self-despair and told I am worthwhile.

We have had a marriage, so we have had hard times. Being religiously mixed has created some storms to weather. We have different viewpoints on priorities and this can be volatile. We have uprooted and started over again three times. And, of course, we have lost a son.

But here we are. Me and my potpourri of little boy, man, lover and best friend. I sometimes get sucked into that meaningless cesspool where I say, "What did I do wrong?" or "Why me? Was I so bad?" But Alan is my verification of self—my proof that somewhere, sometime along the way, I did something very, very good.

Mazeltov to us!

Passion

I haven't let many men into my life—and
even fewer into my heart—but I have a new
love. Alan knows, and he deals with it the
best he can. He understands that when I am
consumed with passion for this person he must retreat to the background and let me play it out.

I have seen my new man only three times,
and each time he changes. His name is Lucas and
he can turn me to jelly with a mere glance of his
big brown eyes. He is in rare company; I can
count on one hand the males who have had this
effect on me.

Our visits are short, and I have to come to
terms with the fact that, although I remember ev-

ery minute of our stolen time together, he will have no conscious memory of my outpouring of love.

When he arrived for his latest visit, he came off the plane in Minneapolis and all I could do was stare. I needed to appraise and reappraise every angle of his face and body. I wanted to soak in his very essence because I knew the clock had begun to tick away on our shared time.

We had planned to see a ballgame together in the Cities but rain changed those plans and we headed for Duluth. I barbecued for him and even fed him. Lucas is a taker and will accept all the attention and pampering that women seem so willing to shower upon him.

We went together to see the fireworks. As the evening wore on, he finally became physical. The very core of my being was yearning to feel his arms around me and his head against my neck. It was wonderful! The warmth of his body pressed close to mine brought back feelings and memories long ago tucked away. The whole experience was sight and sound and feeling and color.

The nights we shared were wondrous. We would lie together sipping warm liquid and stroking each other's face. His hair smelled sweet. His grip was strong. We shared a book and he reached up and held my hair. He never said much, but I knew he was content and that I was meeting his every need.

On Tuesday, we went on a picnic at the lake. The lunch wasn't romantic but it was what he liked. We ate together; he even ate from my fingers. A lovely young girl and her beautiful husky came by. Lucas shamelessly flirted with her. I wasn't hurt because that's Lucas; if you love him, you accept his fickleness. His attention can switch to a thousand things in a day, but it's okay because when he concentrates on you, your world is full of Christmas light.

We romped on the beach, savoring the sensations. He even crawled on the sand and into the cool water.

It was magnificent, and all senses were heightened. The sand was crunchier, the water cooler, the stones smoother and the grass softer than it had ever been before. The world was our oyster as we shared all this and each other.

One day he didn't feel well, and my world trembled. There was selfish solace, though, when he found some peace by resting his head on the rotund mound of my belly or reaching his arms around my neck.

When he was well and smiled again, my heart could have warmed the universe.

The end was fast approaching. Precious time

with him was slipping away. Shopping to be done and no time for intimacy or sharing. And then the trip to Minneapolis and the goodbye. I wanted somehow to make him understand how much I love him.

Then he was leaving and so cavalier about it. I held him, and as he left my arms I cried tears that came from some profoundly empty part of me.

I was promised that he'd be back at Thanksgiving, but he'll be eighteen months old then and will have changed so much.

I know all too well that our sharing will change also, and that in what seems like a blink of time, it will be a cursory hug for Auntie Anne as my grandnephew Lucas goes about life and the living of it.

Dust Bunnies

A s surely as if I have marched up the stairs in Marine-like fashion and planted a flag in the middle of my kitchen floor, I have returned. I have retaken my household after tax season.

I was puttering around the kitchen when Alan walked by, and I said, "Those newspapers are piling up. Could you take them downstairs?" There was an eerie silence and we exchanged glances, both knowing that somehow there had been an unceremonious exchange of roles and that I was once again at the helm of my little ship.

Let me explain that I am not a perfectionist housekeeper; if someone wants to run a white glove test in my home, I can only hope he owns another pair. I like things in their place, relatively dust-free and vacuumed. I am not compulsive, although there are certain things against which I do wage war. Dust bunnies are a prime target. These are big dust bundles that group together and fearlessly float around the corners of my floor until they're big enough to have their own ZIP code.

Generally I'm pretty laid back, but after I take down the Christmas decorations and before I put the furniture back when the tree is gone, I thoroughly clean house. This is because I know that for the next few weeks, during tax season as I prepare returns, a feather duster and dust mop are the best my home can hope for.

This year, my life mate decided he would relieve me of menu planning and cooking. Not only has he been witness to my doing this for twenty-five years, but he comes from good stock. My mother-in-law was an excellent cook and years ahead of her time as far as nutrition goes. She listened faithfully to Dr. Carlton Fredericks on radio and heeded his nutrition tips to reduce sugar and white flour way before it was in vogue. Certainly this man of mine could handle a low-fat cooking plan.

I suppose I had clues that this might not go smoothly, but I was so grateful for his help that I didn't question his efforts.

The recipe called for diced onion. It never occurred to me that he didn't know how to do this. Besides it was no big deal, and real long onion strips are easy to pull out.

Pasta and peppers is a low-fat, meatless favorite. Often I've made this dish with thinly sliced onions and green and red pepper slices, slowly sauteed in a mild tomato sauce. I probably didn't make the "slowly sautéed" part clear, and he wanted to get me dinner between my five-thirty and seven-thirty appointments. So we had pasta and crunchy big pepper chunks. It was fine, even at three a.m. when it made a Mylanta encore. I explained how "raw-ish" peppers were harder to digest. He understood.

The only time I cried was the night of the great chili fiasco.

The man asked if a three-year-old box of minced dried onion was still good. Not knowing, I was noncommittal until I saw the largest amount of dried onion I had ever observed cooking in a skillet. When I found out there were three cups in a recipe for four people, I was doubtful. Naturally it should have been fresh onion. When the dried onion absorbed all the liquid, only a red, grout-like substance was left. That's when I cried.

But this man never lost faith and never stopped trying. He learned that you don't micro-wave the potatoes as Step One to a meal of chicken, potatoes and salad. He learned to appreciate the intricacies of kitchen detail and complimented me on meal planning and meal timing and cooking and working.

So I ignored the goof-ups. And as he called me to dinner each night, and I walked up the stairs, I stopped seeing a kitchen that had every bowl, pot and utensil out and dirty. And I never said a word when the salt shaker was caked with lumpy, yucky stuff.

Toward the end his persistence paid off, and my meals consisted of such foods as cantaloupe, chicken with curry dressing, red cabbage with apple slices and a spinach salad. When you're working so hard and he holds you and says, "I want you to have something special that I did for you," you can't bring yourself to ask where half the pots he's using came from just because you've never seen them before.

Yes, I'm back! Old pots are again hidden and salt shakers are cleaned off. But the onion glue and pepper heartburn and all that went with them are left in the name of total love—and are forever in the corners of the kitchen, keeping company with a dust bunny or two.

My Platform

I agree that athletes' large salaries are deserved because their careers are short, but in perspective, is two million dollars a year not a livable wage?

How about a two million dollar cap for all the athletes, entertainers and CEOs of the world and everything above that to the homeless effort for two years?

There's a platform that assures I'll never be president!

Dickens
of a Time

ickens began A Tale of Two Cities with
these words: "It was the best of times, it
was the worst of times … "
Surely this refers to the period from
Thanksgiving to New Year's.

Everything in these times drips with emotion
and is designed to pluck the heartstrings. And it
works! I cry at every Hallmark commercial, and
the commercials for long-distance telephone service, coffee and the shopping center, too.

Nostalgia washes over me in waves. I think
back to how simple it was to buy gifts for babies.
The presents weren't important; it was the boxes
and wrappings that were the real treat.

Then came the gifts for little boys. Alan and I would stay up 'til wee hours trying to put together race tracks or a riding pelican toy. We would end up, let's say … disgruntled … with one another, before going to bed, and then, in what seemed like only moments, we'd be awakened by cheery and excited children who were eager to open gifts and start the day.

Today's presents are electronic and come in kits that can be assembled only by gifted and talented individuals who, intellectually, are eons ahead of anyone who ever struggled with a riding pelican. As for today's wee hours, that's when the boys go to bed—an occasion that comes long after Alan and I have drifted off. The eye-opening and gift-opening that follow are often instigated by a cheery and excited Mother and are accompanied by brunch, not an early breakfast.

I sit back now and watch it all unfold and think how I used to rush and bustle and put it all together. It made me happy, and it drove me crazy. I love giving gifts, but I hate deciding what to buy. I love the decorations but can't wait until I get my house back to normal.

The tree is always the best we've ever had. Everyone puts it up, and I, alone, take it down.

The ups and downs and highs and lows are built into the season. And, because we in our home celebrate both Hanukah and Christmas, I attempt to make both celebrations memorable. This time of year truly puts us on an emotional roller coaster.

I used to wonder if it was all necessary. My men are not your TV-family types who gush with emotion.

But I know that tradition has been established, and that in their hearts and heads are their expectations of the season. They rely on a sameness to the events of the holidays, and that's good.

I look into my crystal ball and foresee that I will get up early on holiday mornings and begin my kitchen doings. Soon I will have the cooking started, all things organized and the kitchen cleaned. I will be sitting cozily and watching the parade on the television.

Slowly the family will wake up to holiday smells, which will trigger appetites, and the snacking will begin. The parade will vanish from the TV screen, thanks to a remote-control device that apparently is programmed for sports only. Football will begin.

I will retreat to the kitchen, where I will complete a meal that meets everyone's specifications. This involves many factors, not the least of which is onions. One person likes them raw and one likes them cooked and one likes them only when they are diced so they dissolve in the food when cooked.

Then I have to tackle the green things. If this isn't done masterfully, then great amounts of time are spent picking them out of cooked food. This would spell disaster.

Perhaps I haven't mentioned that there is no extra time because all of this food preparation must be orchestrated so the meal is served and consumed to coincide with halftime.

Finally the table is set, the counter is full of steaming holiday fare, I am confident that all onion needs have been met, all green things have been pureed to defy microscopic detection and my family is sitting all together at the same time. This in itself is a miracle.

We don't make a big deal of this experience, however, because halftime is only so long.

But we do express thanks for being together, and we pray for those who are less fortunate.

And, although it is never spoken, we are all painfully aware of the fifth chair that sits empty in the corner.

These are the best of times. These are the worst of times. These are our times, and our times together.

Legacy

We were talking long-distance, as we often do, when my cousin Janice said, "David will graduate law school and has announced his engagement." David is her oldest son, born six weeks after our Steve, and twenty-six years old. Then came the "Are you coming to the wedding?" question. To me!

Wait a minute. This is a matriarch-type question and one always directed at Mama. Who will represent the family at the Sweet Sixteen or the Bar Mitzvah? Who will travel to the graduation or the wedding? It was always Mama going to them, or Aunt Judy coming to us. After all, the youngsters were in school and the young marrieds couldn't afford it or had little children who couldn't travel. But suddenly there I was with the question in my court, and I needed to return the serve.

"Well of course I'll be there. I wouldn't miss it."

This was coming out of my mouth and yet I couldn't help but wonder that I had become old enough. Shouldn't I ask Mama, "Can I go?"

When had I become so free? When had my life evolved to the point of hiring a caretaker for my animals and off I go?

Most of us were at the rehearsal dinner. My sister couldn't make it, but all the rest of us on my mother's side sat and laughed and shared this special moment. Ellen, Cheryl, Jo Susan and Mark are all my mother's brother's children. Janice and Rosalie are Mother's sister Judy's girls. We were a generation grown, with children and all without a living parent. So we were all given a precious gift of togetherness for this wedding weekend.

Cheryl has all the style of her mother. She is two months my junior and has raised two sons. I listened to her talk about not being able to see without her glasses and worrying about her nineteen-year-old, and I remembered that same face flushed from playing cowboys and Indians.

Ellen is elegant and highly educated at forty-four. She leaned to me and said, "I want you to know that your mother was the most non-judgmental person I ever knew. I would love to be even a little like she was." I thanked her even as I recalled that this lovely woman at one time was a whiny tag-along nuisance.

Jo Susan was always a baby in my mind. Yet, at forty, she is a happily married mother of two with great poise and a successful business.

Rosalie was my tiny baby cousin … a kind of toy to me. At forty-four she is a divorcée with two teenage children and struggling to handle all the baggage that comes with her situation. We spoke to each other as women, but inside I wanted to make everything all right because she will always be my baby.

Janice, the mother of the groom, is fifty-two and ageless. As she stood to walk her son down the aisle, I saw her as a bride, and thirty years were gone in the blink of an eye and a trick of the mind.

In fact, there were rips in time all throughout the weekend. I could be on the bottom of a pile of women squeezing in and piling on while laughing uproariously for picture posing, or I could be in the same position as we wrestled on the bed when I came to visit maybe thirty-five years ago. I could be looking into Cheryl's and Ellen's faces and see them forty years earlier as my sister and I used a heater grate in a closet to pretend we had a magic room that produced presents to amaze them.

As I sat there I was dissected, and each surgeon produced a different opinion. "I think she looks like her Daddy around the eyes." "I think she's her Mama from the nose down." "Well I see Judy when she moves her hands." They were all there: Deedum and Papa Joe, our grandparents and their three children and spouses ... Leni and Sy, Robert and Lily, and Judy and Nathan. What functions did they all attend when they were in their forties? What memories did they share of their yesterdays and their children as they grew?

Here we were—the past, present and future—gathered to celebrate as the people on another leaf of the family tree were about to spin off and begin their own life together.

If I had a wish it would be to grab the hands of time and hold on fast and tight. I would want to not let go for fear of getting older and watching those I love get older. This gathering was perfect, and I would have us all as we were, forever.

But if I were to do that, how would our children have their turn? After all, they, too, have foreheads and smiles and hand gestures just like their parents'. They need to have a moment, forty years from now, when they'll discover the pleasure that comes, one day, with knowing that.

Losing A.J.

I've read many articles about long, losing fights with cancer, but until fairly recently I didn't really know what they meant. Now I do. My mother's sister—my Aunt Judy— was diagnosed with cancer about eighteen months ago. After the shock, we in the family were caught up in the swings of emotion—the hope of treatment, the panic of setbacks, the renewed faith from any progress and the torment of defeat. Although we won many battles along the way, in July we lost the war. My "A.J."—Aunt Judy—died.

She and I had a special thing going. She was a bubbly little dynamo who could do anything.

She was my mother's younger sister by about

six years, and she adored Mama. When they were children, A.J. would go to sleep at night only if she could hold Mama's face. (That must have been a magical face, because I remember sleeping best when holding it, as well.)

As a little one, A.J. had curly, red-gold hair. She was a Kewpie-doll type with a fiery temper. She grew up, but changed very little.

The sisters were close. When Mama was in labor with me, it was A.J. she called for, and she made it very clear she would not have this baby without her sister. This was wartime and traveling was no easy feat, but A.J. got there.

A.J. loved her babies and her nieces. The stories of her washing us are well documented. We could not burp, potty or perspire that we were not washed from head to toe.

We lived in Miami and A.J. and her family lived in Tampa. This five-hour trip was made often and before there were good roads between the two cities. Even though we skirted the Everglades and often encountered fog and road hazards, we managed to share the times of our lives.

I especially remember a party my sister had. I was allowed to go, but at the time—the '50s—everyone wore bunches of crinolines and I had none. I cried, and A.J. rescued. She took some of her own and pinned them up under my arms so I could be "pouffy" for the party.

Less than a week later a package came to us in the mail, and inside were two wonderful crinolines made out of some plastic-type material with tiny pink roses on it. I remember the plastic-like stuff, especially, because Mama melted it in the dryer.

I spent many summers with A.J. and her family, and we became friends—even more as the age difference melted away, as it seems to do with the passing of time. I can remember her not being able to sleep and waking me to play cards, which we did all night. Friends can do that.

I remember her trembling chin as I walked down the aisle, and her joy at the birth of my sons. Her children and grandchildren were her life, and she reveled in their achievements. She was a cheerleader for all our triumphs. When we moved from Miami and the football Dolphins to Duluth, her only comment was, "The Vikings! How can you root for the Vikings?"

I can see her face as we buried my son Steven and then six months later as we buried Mama. I think that was her hardest blow.

I always wanted to hear stories. She and I would share them over and over. I always wanted to know more about Uncle this or Aunt that. I loved those moments and am so glad now to have had them. Through these recollections I am able to see family as babies and young people. I know stories of young marrieds and all manner of successes and failures. By sharing, A.J. and I kept generations alive.

Most important, I got to see the wonderful story of two sisters, A.J. and Mama.

A.J. once said, "We were so in tune that one of us could lie and the other would swear to it."

I wish everyone a love like Mama and A.J. shared. I hope you have an Aunt Judy in your own life.

Most of all, pray for me to be able to remember the stories and to have someone to tell them to, over and over again.

Little One

*A*nne, your examination indicates that birth is imminent. Eat light tonight because I expect you'll deliver before morning.

It was October 5, 1973, and Alan's birthday. This baby was due on September 28th, but then Gary had been due on the same date and he had come on October 15th.

I didn't feel the least bit imminent, and, at nine p.m., I had a light portion of a heavy birthday meal—steak, salad and even a small glass of red wine.

It was two a.m. when I woke Alan with those three words that hold the power to move mountains: "Honey, it's time."

The labor room nurse assured us from the fetal heartbeat she could tell that it was a girl and that she was never wrong. Alan and I were delighted that our third offspring would, as the song says, "wear satins and smell of cologne." Well … try denim, sweatshirts and aftershave. At eleven a.m. on October 6, 1973, Joseph was born. The doctor said, "You'll be disappointed about the plumbing, but wait until you see the hair on this one." It was the color of a new penny — a bright copper red.

Joseph, you need to shave. Three days' growth makes your face look dirty, son.

Poor Joe. Unlike his dark-haired brother, Joe doesn't look swarthy when he doesn't shave, and he hates it. "It's that awful red stuff that shows up. Why would I have to have red-hair genes?"

Gary, don't jump on the baby. He's your brother and your friend. Yes, Gary, we are going to keep him!

It was the baby's first birthday, and I made a dozen cupcakes and wrote JOE on each one. The occasion was more a survival party than anything else. I never thought Gary would let Joe get through the year without great bodily harm. Joe, in his highchair, took his cupcake and smashed it into his forehead.

What do you mean by "no fuss" for your birthday? I know you're seventeen and don't need a big thing, but it's my day, too, Joe. I was there, too, so how about a little celebration for me?

A few of the guys over is fine with me, too. Yes, I remember—no cake—because you don't like it.

Will you two please stop fighting! You are not awake ten minutes before you are at each other.

No, you don't hate him. I understand the anger you're feeling, but believe me—you don't hate each other.

Gary, the way you tell me that you keep telling people your little brother is coming … they're going to expect 'Webster Scherer.' Maybe they need to know your 'little brother' played football for his high school.

Well, he is my little brother, but I tell everyone how next year he's going to be a baseball star at Hamline. I tell the St. Thomas ballplayers to enjoy this year because 'Smokin' Joe' is coming.

Why are you boasting so?

Why? Because my baby brother will do so great, and who do you think will be there as his biggest fan? I'm so proud!

Joe, please wear dress pants. Jeans aren't always ap-propriate.

Joe, please wear a jacket. This affair requires more

than a sweater. I know you hate to dress up, but sometimes it's necessary.

Okay—I won't argue any more. Wear what you want.

> The Senior Class
> of Duluth East High School
> Announces its Graduation Ceremony
> Wednesday, June 5, 1991

That's what it said, and I sent it dutifully to friends and relatives alike. They may not know, but I am also announcing that my baby has grown up, and nicely, too. I am announcing that I am pushing the last little one out of the nest to test his wings. My emotions are crossed between total satisfaction in a job done as well as I knew how and growing pains quite different than any a child experiences.

Turn around and you're tiny, turn around and you're grown. How true. I want to yell, "Bring back the years." A thief in the form of time has robbed me of the baby that I still want to cuddle. That same thief says, "Let go." But feelings like these are for me, not Joe.

For him there is only the nectar of anticipation. It is right. It is good.

Carpe diem, Son. Seize the day.

Someday

*D*o you think something's wrong? This baby is three weeks late and I'm worried!

Nothing's wrong, honey. He's just having it his way.

Honey, I think there is something wrong with his foot. It seems to curve.

Anne, he's two days old. Wait and see.

Well, he has pronated ankles, Mrs. Scherer, and a deformed bone in his lower leg. We can't do anything until he walks, but you can try these exercises.

No wonder Uncle Bob calls you 'Smiley.' It's four a.m. and you want to play. Okay, we'll play and do leg exercises and then I'll hold you in my arms and tell you stories of my little baby all grown up someday and very, very happy.

Alan, I can't stand him in those braces. They break my heart. He was so active and now he struggles to do all the things he did before.

Honey, what about when he's sixteen and wants to run and play sports and he can't? Are you going to tell him you could have made him better and didn't? Besides, he is so determined and is just working harder. He doesn't complain at all.

Mrs. Scherer, it's the fastest cure we've ever seen. I expected him in those braces for two years, not just eight months. Watch him closely, but in my opinion, you can throw the braces away. By the way, I think that exercising may have made the difference.

I'm only his sixth grade teacher, Mr. and Mrs. Scherer. But your son has incredible inner drive and a charming sensitivity. He sure does want to learn. He's a real joy.

Let's get you something to do that can be your very own. You think about it.

Are you sure you want to play the drums? Okay, we'll get you started.

He'll need his own snare drum to practice.

You're playing with the Junior Symphony!

He wants a five piece set for his birthday. His teacher said he could get a good price, but they're still very expensive.

Honey, look, his solo got a standing ovation.

You want more cymbals?

Honey, let's move his drums away from the furnace—you know I should dust and cover them.

I was cut from the team. Coach said I wasn't in good enough shape. Baseball is everything. I'm going out.

Where did you go?

I ran, and I'm running every day.

Esther, I'm so glad you and Bob could come for his graduation and be here for the baseball banquet, too.

Esther, look, the coach is crying.

Some goodbyes are very hard. This young man has more drive and character than any his age. As a sophomore I cut him from the varsity squad just days after his brother's death, but his determination brought him here tonight. It's indeed hard to say goodbye to our starting varsity third baseman.

Turn around and you're grown ...

I'm going to graduate college with honors just like high school. I promise, ranked Number One!

Well, I made the Dean's List.

I'll be home this summer to coach a Little League team. By the way, I met a girl.

Something is getting closer and closer. I can't name it, but I feel it bearing down on both of us.

I passed my second actuarial exam. I won't be home this summer. I got a job at a bank.

Here it comes again.

Three companies, can you believe it! They all want me for a summer internship.

I can't believe it. I'm an actuary—I'm so excited that nothing could bring me off Cloud Nine. Just think, I'll graduate Magna Cum Laude in December and I'm almost assured of a good job.

That's it, I know what's been coming. Why didn't I see it before? It was someday, and it's here. The time when Mommy's little baby will be all grown up and very, very happy!

Turn around and you're a young man going out on your own.

God speed, Gary. God speed!

Red Corvair

We were sitting in a red Corvair, outside my house, and we were young, engaged and very much in love. We talked about our future together and how we would have our children while we were still young. We went on with a most cavalier air about the time when they would all be gone and we would still be in our prime and be able to travel and cavort and most of all enjoy each other.

Well, we are now staring that far-away future square in the eyes and I, for one, have never felt so old.

I recently went to a local moving company to get boxes. I had been there twice before, when our older sons moved from home to school, but this trip was for the baby who would now leave the nest.

I am the orchestrator of this departure. I meticulously make lists that are titled by child and then are broken into finite categories such as: Bath/Shaving Needs; Bed/Linen Needs; Desk/Room Needs. There are five major headings and six sub-categories. It is pure genius.

The reaction of the boys is best described as overwhelmed. My older boy, Gary, told his younger brother, "There is nothing Mommy bought me that I didn't need."

Now I'm feeling pretty smug even though there's a nagging thought in the back of my mind: "Then how come his dental floss, Q-tips and iron seem relatively untouched?"

Joe was looking through his stuff and held up a bottle, asking, "What's this for? I've never taken Pepto Bismol in my life." What I had to make him understand was that even if he never needed it and even if he never took it, it was there for him, and that's security! Finally the child was beaten down and listened intently to why he needed things he had never heard of before.

Joe will attend Hamline University in St. Paul while his brother Gary goes to St. Thomas. Hamline and St. Thomas start classes on September 4. Joe, however, has a three-day orientation period beginning on the first. Parents are also included. From nine to five on the first there are joint activities. Then at five p.m. the schedule says, "Family Farewell." I ask you, is this necessary? I can think of a hundred better phrases than that one! But, no matter how it's put, we will leave our baby Joseph in the hands of the big university monster.

We are having dinner that night with Gary and his ladyfriend. On Monday, the second, Gary can move into his dorm at one p.m. So by three-thirty he should be settled, passing out hand-shakes, hugs and kisses and wishing we would move on out.

By eight o'clock that night we should be home.

I am forty-five and for twenty-three years, more than half of my life, I have been a hands-on mom. By that I mean I knew where my children were and who they were with pretty much all the time. Now I will know only what they choose to share with me. It is natural that they take control and responsibility of their lives, and I know that Alan and I have done all we could and that they should make good choices. But for now my new role is a little undefined, a little too new and a little painful.

We were sitting on the couch in our home

and we were young, married twenty-four-plus years and very much in love. We talked about our future together with the boys gone and us in our prime.

"Will you watch football on TV with me?" he asked. "Yep," I replied.

"Will we still go watch high school sports together?" he asked. "Yep," I replied.

"You know the boys may not call a lot. Will you be okay?" he asked. "Yep, I guess," I replied.

"Think how full the house will be when they're home for the holidays!" he said.

"Yep. It will be exciting," I replied.

"With two in school, we really can't afford to travel but we could take a walk," he said.

"Yep," I replied. "But could we maybe get silly and cavort?"

It should be fun to see the many ways we will enjoy each other—now that we're alone, young and in love—everything according to plan.

Visitation Rites

My cup runneth over. As the holidays approached I was buoyed by the fact that for the first Thanksgiving in eleven years, I would have family visiting.

The boys would be home, which was, in itself, exciting. In addition, my sister, brother-in-law and their grandson were coming for a visit. That grandson is my godchild, and I have not seen him since he was a few weeks old. He is now a ripe old eight months.

You may wonder why his mother would let him take this trip. First, she loves me very much, and, second, I never quite forgave her for drinking all my perfume when she was a little girl. I figured that guilt would come in handy some day. But I wander from the topic. The Visit.

My sister and I are very different people. She dwells on little details and tends to make mountains out of molehills. She is a worrier beyond belief. I have trouble coming to terms with us being from the same gene pool because I ignore small stuff and am totally removed from fanaticism. I may worry, but it has to be a worry-worthy issue. Let me explain further.

As The Visit date drew closer, the phone calls increased and with each one I could hear more and more concern in my sister's voice. I had to chuckle as I tried to keep her calm. "Do you have any hooded towels?" she asked. "No, but I have big towels we can wrap around his head—just relax."

When we hung up I was amused by my sister being herself. I guess I was amused until two a.m., when I awoke, wondering where I was going to wash this baby. The kitchen sink is cold, the bathroom sink is small and the tub is on the floor.

In another call she asked, "What should I do about dressing the baby? After all, we are leaving in eighty-degree weather."

Boy, she can worry! "We'll bundle up at the airport," I said. She really tickles me, that girl. It was much later when "bundle up" hit home. In what?

I needed to borrow a bunting and a snowsuit and sweaters and hats and blankets. I scrounged through my packed-away baby treasures and washed until the wee hours.

Boy that girl can worry. "Buy Stage Two baby food," she said. "And get some tropical fruit flavors, like guava." Guava? "And buy Pampers for boys." For boys? All these details!

I'm glad I can rise above it all and just relax and enjoy a visit. However, I did notice that the beams in my laundry room were dusty, so I vacuumed the rafters. You never know when someone will look up.

While I was searching for baby things, I decided it was a good time to rearrange my entire linen closet. And, one good look and anyone would know that the pantry needed organizing. Then there's my room, which is always Christmas Central at this time of year. Well, the baby would sleep there so I had to re-do drawers and closets and shelves.

It is amazing how one sister like mine and one little tiny baby could cause so much activity. That's what I blame it on—it can't possibly be genes because, as I said, my sister and I are such very different people.

Get No Kick

Iwas listening to a radio commercial that said, "Treat Mother as she deserves to be treated … with berries, crepes and champagne on her special day."

I had to laugh, and my mind was visited by the Ghost of Mother's Days Past. I could hear the rustle of little people in the kitchen as I lay in bed. I could see the beaming faces as I was handed orange juice, a roll and cream cheese.

Once I got something that I'm pretty sure was an egg. I do know, however, that some things can lie dormant in your body for years, and every once in a while I get a strange pain and wonder about that egg.

Soon those young people became teenagers and realized that Mother's Day would always come on Sunday, which would follow Saturday night, and that made that early morning breakfast in bed stuff very overrated. So they brought in the big guns, in the form of … "Daddy." Now I get melon, orange juice, a roll and cream cheese.

The boys are older now—and this special day has taken on a new nature. In the past my gifts could be anything, but now I usually get what I ask for. Maturity does that, I guess.

This year it was a desk lamp. It was presented unwrapped with a used Christmas bow stuck on top of the box.

I opened the box and took out not just a desk lamp but an initial pin from an eight-year-old— the initial was "M" for Mommy. I took out a mug with "World's Best Mom" on it. Next came a four-year-old's handprint forever in clay, and then stuffed animals and handmade cards and little boys scrambling into bed with me.

It was Mother's Day, and my gift was the memories.

Time may have changed the format, and my men certainly bumble the pomp and frills, but I do get unsolicited hugs and kisses. Now, tell me, who needs crepes and champagne?

M

When I die—which I hope doesn't happen until sometime after the first black, Jewish and woman presidents have been elected—who will take care of my "M"?

As I sit here, thankfully quite alive, I wonder about the things I treasure, my "M" being one of them. I do not sit around and dwell upon my demise, but certain events have brought thoughts of it to the forefront lately.

For example, Joey has been getting ready for football. He has been running and lifting weights all summer. One result of all this activity is a waist that went from thirty-three to thirty-two inches.

When we discovered this, I suggested that he try on his late brother Steve's jeans, which were still on a shelf. He said that he had but that they were not in style.

At about the same time, Gary called from the Cities and said he could use a new comforter. His old one was worn and not puffy and had holes. It had been Steve's.

While still home, Joe went to have a tape deck installed in the used car we bought him. The tape deck had been salvaged from Steve's first car. Steve had bought a top-of-the-line tape player, and when his car was junked he said to be sure and save the tape deck. Joe marched into the installation shop with this seven-year-old unit and was made to feel foolish because it was so outdated. He bought a golf club instead.

Obsolescence is scary. But it did make me think. I was there to save or pass on those things that were once important to Steve, but who would even know about *my* things, especially my "M"?

I remember when Mama died and my sister and I had to go through her things. I felt like an intruder. I was touching things she had kept forever because of what they meant to her; to me, most of them meant nothing. I did not want the responsibility of keeping or discarding the mementoes of her life.

So that is the whirlwind of events and reminiscing that brings me to the need to declare which material things are precious to me. When I go, there will be a lot of clutter to go through, with school pictures and drawings and baby shoes and a wedding veil. However, before they seal me up (remember not to rush this), please keep this in mind:

I have received hundreds of love letters and notes from Alan and each one is special. However, the very first one is most precious. I was at Florida State University and Alan was at the University of Miami. We were apart two weeks and I was miserable. I had sent letters and cards and got nothing back. Finally, I got an eight-page letter from my future husband that foretold what the next umpteen years of my life would be. The first seven and a half pages were a detailed account of a great softball game he had played. The last half page was about loving me more than anything else.

Next is a pink silk rose with a battery case on the stem. We were at Valley Fair—the whole family and Steve's girlfriend. They were selling roses that twinkled via battery power. Steve and his girl walked up with one. It was for me, from Steve, with a hug and kiss. It sits on my dresser.

Third is a stuffed Dumbo that Gary bought me. He went with the band to Los Angeles in his junior year of high school. His spending money allowed for a souvenir for Joe and several for himself, but not much else. When he came home he was so proud to bring me Dumbo, and it had a twelve-dollar price tag—quite a sacrifice.

In my jewel box is a little plastic oyster shell. If you open it you will find all the baby teeth the tooth fairy bought. I don't know whose is whose anymore, and no one would want them anyway. But you can't throw out baby teeth.

Last, in preparation for Mother's Day many, many years ago, the boys went shopping for me. They were on their own at the mall and each proudly purchased his choice. I don't remember the other gifts, but have kept and proudly worn Joey's. He bought me an enameled pin that resembles a rainbow and has an initial on it. His brothers made fun of him but he didn't back down one inch. The initial on the pin is "M," for Mommy.

That would be all I'd take with me. I don't know what I'd leave behind, but I will offer this advice:

Try not to keep things that belonged to your loved one. It hurts to watch as they become time-worn.

Memories, however, are ageless and always in style, and they never wear out.

Plans

*A*bsolutely nothing could change our plans. We had been surging toward the completion of a goal, and we would not be denied.

On Wednesday, April 14, Alan and I would finish our tax returns. On Thursday, April 15, I would take care of return pickups, extension filers and business sales tax reports for my clients.

On Friday, April 16, I would have a long-overdue haircut. On that evening I would attend a party given by the accounting firm I have worked for. On Saturday, April 17, Alan and I would drive to the Cities to see a ballgame of Joe's and visit with Gary.

And on Sunday, April 18, I would spend the entire day … every minute, every second … relaxing—reading and TV watching and feet up-putting. In the following week, Alan and I would go away for a few days. These plans were etched in stone, with appointments and R.S.V.P.s and reservations and confirmations. The tax season and its sixteen- and eighteen-hour days require this kind of carrot on a stick to get you through.

Alan and I do our own taxes in a unique manner. Early in the season, when I have time, I make worksheets listing income and expenses, based on receipts I have kept. Around March, Alan makes worksheets of income and expenses based on canceled checks. On our Tax Night, we match our worksheets and I fill out our IRS forms.

That's where we were, filling out tax forms, when at about eight-thirty p.m. the phone rang for the umpteenth time that day. I answered and listened to the message and then called to my husband. With sadness and tears I said, "Honey, I'm so sorry, but your mother has just died."

The next hour was a frenzy of phone calls to our boys and Alan's aunt and his stepbrothers and my sister and the hospital, funeral home, travel agent and car rental.

Alan had to work the next morning and I had sales tax returns to prepare but my secretary could reschedule and his secretary could reschedule, and then of course we had to call and cancel and cancel and cancel.

My mother-in-law was 85, blind and losing her faculties. She had a noncancerous brain tumor that was growing, but at a pace that no one could predict. Her prognosis was for deterioration over time into death. She chose to have a quick heart attack in her home and go with dignity and style. Thus her death was not a tragedy in many respects. But it was another painful goodbye in an altogether too long list of goodbyes.

I am sitting in her home in New Jersey. I am sitting at her place at her table. I am watching my husband as he writes the words he will speak at her funeral.

I am conjuring up images of her life as it became part of mine, and it is as though I'm building a kaleidoscope of Elsie the woman, the mother, the grandmother, the sister, the church member. She is in memory as she was in life, a special lady.

I also am thinking of set-in-concrete plans that vanished in a moment when the only real plan, life's plan for us, surfaced. I am reminded that the only sure things, bet-on-it things, etched-in-stone things are death and taxes. And suddenly it isn't a funny punch line anymore.

Black Hole

I don't know about other refrigerators, but on every shelf of mine is a certain point beyond which lurks the Black Hole. Once an object reaches that point it is as good as gone. In desperate times, say when the chips are gone, someone in my household will actually reach in there. I don't know why. Even the most desperate individual has to know that whatever might be retrieved will be neither edible nor recognizable. Inevitably I will be asked, "What is this?" I don't ever know what it is, or used to be. However, I do know that it makes no difference because now it is blue-green and hairy, with puffy white accents. Next time I'm asked, I'll yell: "STOP! I got a federal grant to grow that!"

When Lilacs Bloom

Out of Whack

*I*ncongruous ... that's what it all is ... incongruous. I looked it up: "Being inappropriate or out of place."

I am all alone tonight. Normally I am okay with this and occasionally even welcome being alone. Tonight, however, I am uncomfortable. Maybe it's because Alan took Joe to St. Paul for a college recruiting dinner; later they will spend time with Gary at St. Thomas.

I have been with tax clients from eight-thirty this morning until eight-thirty this evening, and yet I am lonely. Maybe "left out" is closer to what I am feeling.

I feel the need to reflect. In most years I am

forced by the tax business to postpone my reflections until April 16. Tonight, though, as if a force is pulling me, I take a June lawn chair out into a February night and gaze at the winter sky.

It makes me sad that I have never mastered sky-watching and cannot pick out the constellations, and even sadder because I had hoped to see Jupiter.

If I did find Jupiter I didn't know it, However, I did feel as though I was talking with a friend. I knew that in some galaxy somewhere there had to be a life form out there that night who also was hoping to see his or her Jupiter equivalent.

I wondered why I was able to sit and gaze and enjoy these far-fetched yet warm thoughts while half a world away no one was stargazing; instead they were running from bombs, running for shelters and grabbing for gas masks.

My mind turned to the Gulf War that was going on then. I thought of expressions that we learned in those few weeks—phrases that now roll off our tongues like cocktail-party prattle.

Like "friendly fire." Oh, I understand what the military means by the expression, and I can believe that in the heat and fear of battle that friendly fire is, as they tell us, inevitable. It's hard to accept nonetheless. I saw a friendly-fire widow on TV. No, the results didn't look friendly.

I thought of "smart bombs." I wondered if that meant that the bombs knew not to kill civilians and terrorize the skies of innocent people. Again on the TV, I saw an Iraqi woman shaking her finger and spewing hatred at us for the fear that she and her family and friends live with. I don't want her to hate me. Even when we begin to pour endless dollars into her country to rebuild the destruction I will remain the "Ugly American."

I thought of the picture I saw of an old Israeli man being lifted from the rubble of a Scud-missiled building. What a way to spend your golden years. I don't want people old or young to live with these horrible memories.

I remember that when I was in elementary school, in the fifties, we had bomb drills. We practiced getting under our desks until the hypothetical danger was over. It was scary, even for pretend.

I wonder what the children of this war … who run for cover into shelters and carry lunch pails and gas masks … who cry because a parent or other relative is gone … who are so scared—I wonder what they will carry as memories and what damage has been done to them.

I wonder if the president will keep his promise not to reinstate the draft better than he kept his read-my-lips promise not to raise taxes.

I think of the whole picture. That when the

bands stop playing we will be left with cold statistics of the prisoners, the missing and the dead.

I wonder if my galactic life-form buddy knows of war and worries for his or her child, and all children. I feel so alone, as if I am the only one pondering the awfulness of it all.

My night was to have been so simple. I went out to stargaze but was blinded by the light of bombs bursting in air, half a world away.

It is incongruous ... as incongruous as a June lawn chair in a February night.

Anne's Place

I am wishing for a place of my own. Not a home—I have that. I mean a place. There's a lyric in a song from the musical My Fair Lady where Liza sings, "All I want is a room somewhere … now wouldn't that be loverly?"

I'm not an escapist. I face life rather squarely. For me, escape is usually losing myself in a really good book. But lately, I find myself like the philosopher Diogenes, who spent his lifetime looking for an honest man. I am looking for a place with no "scams" and no "gates." A place where you don't feel that every action is driven by ulterior motives.

Every day we are presented with a new government plan only to see it blocked because of one item it contains that some Congressperson can't endorse.

This is the process, but when it causes nothing to change, then "we the people" despair. And when we examine the motives, we wonder and despair even more.

For example, some in Congress propose to be against the president's energy tax because it would hurt the farm community. On the surface it sounds noble, but are they really carrying a banner and caring about farmers, or are the brakes on change because the real motive is getting the farmers' votes?

It has come to the point where I question whether those who push the buttons on the machinery of government have any burning issues and unselfish passions. What I fear is that they are all puppets dangling from the strings of lobbyists and special-interest groups.

What else could be behind favoring a patch of people when they are but a part of the whole Americana quilt covering us all? This mistrust is forced upon us when we are treated to stories of lobbyists paying for extravagant vacations for our lawmakers.

What else, when senators and lobbyists are best friends and together participate in a telephone scandal that ultimately casts yet another cloud of doubt on our government? What else, when the White House transportation committee is accused of misrepresenting facts, mishandling money and monopolizing opportunity, thus squashing free enterprise?

What else, when nepotism is used as a problem's solution? The highest office in the land has to be free of suspicion and therefore has no room for it.

These are leaders who then have to deal with issues that touch us all: unemployment, taxes, drugs, AIDS, abortion.

And then there's the issue of "To war or not to war" in Bosnia. These people in our government, who seem to be bought and sold, hold our lives in the palm of their hands. No wonder that a person with some charisma can rise up and promise truth and solutions and "the way" and gain followers who would die for him. Our government and the media, who spoonfeed us their ugliest features, are a breeding ground for cult movements such as the Branch Davidians.

Do I think the country has gone to hell in a hand basket? Hardly. But by now we must all be looking for someone whose motives are unquestionable to stand up and yell, "Stop!"

I think all Americans should submit a list of what they believe the country's greatest needs are and what they are willing to do to meet them.

Then, these should be put in order of priority and a hand-picked group of Americans should see that the needs are met. No lobbyists would be required since this would be our mandate, every person's say included.

It will never happen, I agree, so I'll continue to look for my place. A cabin in the woods, a place on a lake, an island in the sea. It doesn't matter, as long as everyone there says what he or she means, and that they mean what they say, and care. Really care.

Her Highness

The first election night that I remember was exciting and electric. We had dinner and then all gathered around the radio to listen as results came in. There were no early projections then, and we went to bed before all the West Coast results were reported. It was thrilling, and I just knew Adlai Stevenson would win. After all, my mother and my father thought he was the best candidate, and surely the nation would go the way of my parents.

The next day's papers said Stevenson was a brilliant man but that he was before his time and that the nation liked Ike.

By the time of the next election–night coverage we had switched to television. Again the nation was not swayed by my parents. Stevenson was still before his time, and the country still liked Ike.

These days election night is not exciting. It is merely an exercise to fulfill the prophecies of the election soothsayers who tell us weeks, days and hours before we vote who will win. But if my family were the only survey base from which to extrapolate results, the picture would be a little cloudy.

Alan is a Republican. He is concerned with social issues but is most concerned with interest rates. He is paralyzed with fear of rampant recession.

Gary is impressed that his candidate took time to appear on MTV. His favorite addressed the eighteen- to thirty-year age group and expressed his cares about their economic fears coming out of college and looking for a job.

Joe is a bottom-line young man. He is not impressed by outdated mudslinging and banter. He is a "damn the torpedoes and full speed ahead" kind of kid. So a man with no time for campaign rhetoric and a warp-speed action plan is his cup of tea.

It appears, then, that the entire election rests on my shoulders.

Well, at eighteen I was a fiery, outspoken,

die-hard Democrat. And through my twenties I was pretty much the same liberal, idealistic voter. In fact, this is the first year I'm analyzing my voting self. I'm doing this because working, paying bills, raising kids, struggling and just aging make holding on to all of youth's idealism a little like holding on to a cloud.

I'm not in love with any candidate. I, too, am scared of soaring interest rates and high unemployment. But I can't stand ignoring social needs and letting our own countrymen and women suffer while feeding foreign coffers. I also understand that foreign markets need to be economically healthy to buy our exports. I don't want to see income taxes raised for the middle class, but I could suggest a surtax on the very wealthy and a repeal to taxing unemployment benefits, which is basically a middle-class tax.

As for military spending, if I'm eighteen or eighty I will always consider war the filthiest of all four letter words. (Not a Dan Quaylism; I can spell, and count!)

I read recently about the Sultan of Brunei. This guy is the absolute monarch of a small but incredibly oil-rich country. He has an estimated wealth of thirty-seven billion dollars and had just been carried though the streets in a gold encrusted chariot to celebrate the twenty-fifth year of his reign. I had little use for this man, but the article continued with why his 261,000 subjects came out to wave at him.

In Brunei there is no income tax, no national debt and no trade deficit. And the budget always shows a surplus. Education, medical care and pensions are free and no-interest loans are provided for cars and houses.

Think what a great platform that is for a candidate. Whatever comes from the earth—whether it be oil, jewels, or minerals—belongs to the people and goes back to the people. The initial finders of these treasures will receive ten percent of all profits, which will make them wealthy. This is the mother lode of all great ideas.

But I have pollsters waiting for me to cast my vote and break the Scherer family deadlock. Okay. I shall tell everyone that all our problems can be solved if we share in the bounties of Mother Earth. So, pollsters, I cast my ballot for Anne Scherer as absolute monarch and Sultaness of America.

I hope the press doesn't think my ideas are before my time.

Miss Daisy

H er name was Gussie, but all seven grandchildren called her "Deedum." I'm told
that's how "Grandma" tumbled out of
the eldest grandchild's mouth.

Deedum's family were Russian immigrants.
She was the only one born in America. Because
her family had seen so much oppression, Deedum
had no tolerance for bigotry in any form.

In the early 1940s in Birmingham, Alabama,
the black woman who worked for Deedum was
standing in the kitchen, eating lunch and drinking
from a jar. Deedum was appalled and insisted that
the woman sit at the table and drink from a glass.

The woman was afraid of the overture and only slowly acquiesced.

A neighbor stopped in and saw the scene. She said, "Gussie, you allow that girl at your table and you'll never again have a friend at your home."

Deedum said, "Of course I will. I'll have the girl."

This memory is churning inside me as I watch the movie Driving Miss Daisy.

The movie's story takes place in the South from 1948 to 1973. The movie is about a beautiful friendship that grows between two people. In addition, it deals with prejudice and the South in those years.

Most of the filmgoers around me are too young to remember those times, or were an arm's length away from the turmoil that took place. But I was there then. And I was there again as I watched the film. It sent memories and visions swirling all around me.

Mama was a caterer, and among her helpers were some black women. One special lady was Laurie, who became Mama's friend. Daddy called her "Big Feet." Laurie stayed at the house to prepare the food after Daddy was buried, and she cried as she said, "Who's gonna call me Big Feet anymore?"

To her, a friend was gone; a colorless friend. I was only twelve. The memories are so vivid.

It was the fifties and we were in Florida. In a department store I saw that one water fountain was marked "White" while the other was marked "Colored." I asked Mama why. She said, "People can be ignorant, but you can make a difference." I promised I would try.

The flashbacks are jumbled and out of order. As I watched the film something triggered my memory bank and visions popped in and out of my mind.

I was on a bus, and blacks were required to sit in the back. I took my first step toward changing things when I took my seat … in the back. It was the sixties and I was a teenager ready to make a difference, confident that I would change the world.

In the movie, Miss Daisy says to her son that something has been stolen and refers to how "those people" steal. Her son says she is a bigot, and she says she most definitely is not.

"Those people." How I hated the stereotypes.

I traveled all over with a message that it was okay not to like someone, but not simply because of what color they were or religion they believed in. I felt so deeply. I was so passionate to be heard.

I would march with Dr. King to show my belief in nonviolent change. I was sixteen and I wanted change—now!

Twenty-eight years after the fact I wonder if Mama worried about me when I went off to march—or if I would let my boys do that today. But she knew I had to act on my beliefs.

Miss Daisy is being driven to synagogue and is held up by traffic and police. She discovers that her temple had been bombed. I remember those bombings.

I guess I was five when I realized that not everyone was Jewish, but it was much later when I discovered what it meant to be Jewish. It was eighth grade, and I had gone to sharpen my pencil. When I got back there was a note on my desk: "Beware, Jew Girl!"

It hurt and confused me so badly then, and now, thirty-two years later, I sit in a theater crying from the pain of wondering why he hated me.

I was at Florida State University and it was 1965. The picture I put on my dresser was of my sister's wedding. The men in the picture wore yarmulkes, or skullcaps. Why were all the girls whispering and huddled away from me? Finally, Sonia, my roommate from a backwoods dot on the map known as Auburndale, Florida, said, "Are you Jewish?" She wanted to feel the horns on my head. I didn't laugh or hurt; instead, I taught them about me and my people. We shared Passover together that year.

Dreams of the Peace Corps turned into marriage, night school and many, many diapers.

My son was young when he asked to bring home his best friend. He had talked of him incessantly, but we were surprised to discover the friend was black. It didn't mean enough to Steven for him to mention it. We had raised our boys prejudice-free. Bigotry was dead on our tree branch.

In the movie, Miss Daisy attends a dinner at which Dr. King is speaking. We hear an excerpt. He says that bigotry is not just what is apparent and out in the open; it is also, and perhaps worse, people who are confronted with prejudice and do nothing.

We moved to this Nordic ethnic area and my dark-skinned, dark-haired boy begged me to do nothing when he heard, "Hey, Pablo!" I agreed.

I was between "thirtysomething" and fortyish and I heard basketball described as "nigger hockey." I said nothing.

Another of my sons had a yearbook in which almost every autograph referred to his Jewishness. He said it was friendly and meant nothing. I said it did.

I was told that the expression "Jew it down" was common among high schoolers. I didn't make an issue.

After all the years of leading, teaching, marching and torch bearing, I was being silent. I had made a difference and let it die. The convictions lived on, but the courage of those convictions got lost and buried.

But no more. Thanks to Miss Daisy. After all, I promised Mama.

Judge Not

*H*ello, my name is Anne, and I'm morbidly obese." Is anyone out there applauding me because I've admitted to having a problem? I doubt that.

More than any other circumstance, being heavy subjects a person to ridicule every day of his or her life, and from life's earliest stages. By the time we are young adults, we have been told by family, friends, the unkind and the media that to be worthy is to be thin—that appearance is the measure by which we are judged.

So we diet. We watch calories and fat grams and portions. And we walk and run and bike and dance and stretch. Our self-esteem has become so interwoven with this issue that to fail with weight control is to fail ourselves and the people who love us.

Food is an enemy, and yet a necessity: We must eat to live.

And beyond nutrition, food is part of our social life. With food we celebrate, congratulate and console. Food is everywhere, but the obese are seen as people who are unable to control their appetites. We are stereotyped as clumsy, lazy and weak-willed.

I am none of those. I was an excellent dancer before I felt too big to dance. I put in twenty-hour days seven days a week during the tax season. I quit a three pack a day cigarette habit cold-turkey.

We overweight people work just as hard as normal people. I can scrub floors, paint and wallpaper a room or do yard work.

I also can sit and read for hours. My activities are limited only by the fact that—according to the weight charts—every time I get up from my reading, I lift an extra hundred and twenty pounds. I would love to have one of my hecklers try that a few times.

Yes, I get tired and my leg hurts, but I don't give in. Not that there aren't discouraging moments: Even the obese people on my exercise tape seem to have and easier time than I.

Oprah Winfrey has done wonders with her body. She has been told that she has low metabolism, so she has a trainer come twice a day to work with her, hands-on. She has a cook make delicious meals, prepared just for her body's needs.

Oprah makes ninety-six million dollars a year. I don't. So I have to worry about fat grams and portion size and calorie content. We all do, but I am judged as a person on whether I succeed or fail.

The Duluth daily newspaper recently carried a story about a woman who was denied employment because she was excessively overweight. According to the story, she had passed a physical and had previously done the job. A court ruled that her weight was a disability over which she was powerless and that she had an underlying condition rooted in a defective metabolism.

(I contend that many excessively obese people have defective metabolisms. I take Thyroid, which means I can lose weight, but only slowly and with difficulty.)

The paper ran an editorial after publishing the story and claimed to be totally against the fat bias demonstrated by the woman's employer. The last paragraph of the editorial ran as follows: "Should all obesity be considered a disability? No, it should not. ... Where that condition can be proved [defective metabolism], then such obesity should be considered a disability. However, people should not be able to eat themselves into disability status consciously. To allow that would invite abuses."

I have never read anything that displayed a greater lack of insight into the problem of obesity or that displayed more fat bias than that paragraph.

The thin world has no idea how prevalent weight prejudice is and how hard stereotypes die.

All we can do is try to lose weight for our health and not for someone else's definition of who we are.

The next time you're tempted to stare at or laugh at or chide obese people, consider that maybe this was the day they chose to be normal and not think about being fat. Give them that opportunity.

Joys of Summer

*I*am sitting at a picture window and gazing at the Mississippi River as it rolls between its banks. It is as though it has been lifted from song and book and laid in my lap. Because of the view, I feel as if I should be writing something worthy of Mark Twain—powerful and clear —but I am lost in a sea of images that I want to share.

I am in St. Cloud at a baseball tournament for my younger son's VFW team.

From March until August we are professional baseball parents. We huddle in winter coats and blankets; sit through rain and hail storms; swelter, fry and burn; fight mosquito, fly and bee; and travel at a moment's notice.

There are double- and triple-headers. They add up to bleacher-sitting for hours. This year a game began at eight on Tuesday and ended after midnight on Wednesday.

Why endure this? Well, mine are boys of summer. We all love the sport, and for me, after a combined forty-four hours of labor to have three sons, I deserve to get all the accolades I receive when they do well. So I shiver and drip and sweat and swat and travel … after all, it's summer.

The river is moving slowly and truly lazily rolling along. It knows it is "summertime and the livin' is easy…" It is a time of freedom from heavy clothing and heavy cooking and inflexible schedules. This is when iced tea becomes a heavenly nectar and the backyard fills with the aroma of barbecue and the sounds of volleyball and softball and the joy of harvesting the tomato from the vine I planted. I read recently that this summertime is on borrowed time and about to take a final curtain call … to which I say: "Bah, humbug!"

There's still a summer picnic in this old girl. A time when I and food and nature all meld as though embracing.

I'm not ready to bid farewell to an easy hour of lazily bathing in sunshine with my nose in a novel that takes me far away and cloaks me in intrigue. Nor have I reached my quota of castles and horses and islands that I find in the clouds as they float in the sky.

And I haven't relived all my summertime memories. They are burned into the soul, and a smell or sound brings a memory back and suddenly my sister and I are running through the summer sand into the ocean. We listen but don't hear as Mama runs through her list of "be careful not to's."

There is absolutely nothing like the combination of salt water, sand, sun, suntan oil and sandwiches.

Now I'm fishing. "Don't look, Anne," they tell me. They want me to be surprised by my catch. I have spent hours with my uncles on their boat drifting on the Gulf of Mexico. They are determined that I, too, catch a fish before we go in.

It finally happens and I can still feel the triumph.

No gold medalist has ever felt more.

(It would be years later before I found out I had snagged some treacherous form of catfish and, while I wasn't looking, they had let it go. I dined on fish that night caught another time by a different fisherman, but I thought the fish was mine and none has ever tasted better.)

So many summers were spent with my cousins in Tampa. We would go crabbing. It was always a perfect blend of fun and family and the catch. I promise to tell you someday of the time sixty live crabs got loose in my aunt's house. For now maybe you can picture women on chairs screaming, a dog running around barking and men with crab nets trying to recatch—not from warm waters, but from behind a stereo or under a couch —some very angry crustaceans.

Summertime is almost over! It can't be. Summer is more than a time; it is a happening and a symphony of the senses. And, as the song says, "They can't take that away from me." Especially as I sit here watching the river as it sunbathes and I am moments away from hearing an umpire say the immortal, "Play ball!"

This is summertime.

Sunbeams

*I*n this height of the tax season I spend most of my time in my basement office.

I am completely surrounded by tax returns in various stages of readiness—"to be prepared," "to be copied" and "to be picked up."

I see countless people, and I intimately enter their lives for an hour or so. We laugh and cry and solve world problems. For sixteen weeks my basement headquarters is quite exciting, with comings and goings and deadlines and conquering what seems, at times, the impossible.

There is a change, though, as the end of March and the beginning of April approach.

The people are still wonderful, but now there

is sunshine streaming into my office. The emotions we share are still great, but when I look out I can see buds on the lilac bush and tulips beckoning to spring's call. The tax work is still challenging, but even a tax accountant's fancy can turn to thoughts of spring.

I have a client who, to say the least, is an outdoors enthusiast. He says that getting the mail is an outdoors experience for me. We laugh, but he's not too far from right.

So, one day I took a real outdoors excursion and walked around the house. I discovered a crack under my bedroom window and paint peeling in the back of the house and my large evergreens badly damaged by the heavy snow. And, between the Arctic Cat that finally plowed my driveway in November and the excavating crew that dug up my lawn in two places to remove a root from my clogged sewer line, my front yard looks like a missile testing site. The outdoors experience was not going well, so I sat on my back steps and just soaked the outside in.

I began to marvel at the peace one can find in watching things grow. This experience reduces things that may be wrong to a lower mark on the scale of importance. I thought of the vernal equinox and how this event is so subtly accomplished for something so grand. There is a real lesson there—to be great, one doesn't need fanfare.

Yep, sitting and watching things bud is heavy stuff. I also heard birds singing. They were ready for new beginnings and very forgiving of the harsh winter gone by. They were also quite at home in the cracked, peeling and missiled environment I provided them. Perhaps having a home, even one needing care, is still better than having no home at all. My excursion changed my outlook.

On the day I chose for my adventure I was dwelling on endings, and it was refreshing to get some perspectives on beginnings as plants grew and creatures returned home to sing. It is amazing what you can see when you're not looking and learn when you're not trying.

I decided to walk around the house again and look at things differently. The crack was certainly fixable, and the peeling—well, there was still some house paint left to touch it up after scraping. The bushes were in bad shape, but we have needed a tree service to trim the shrubbery for years—it would be a real treat. And the yard. It *is* awful and still looks like a missile testing site, and I have little hope there. But three out of four is pretty good for one excursion.

It is nice to bring some springtime in as I go back to my basement office and draw comfort from the sunbeams that stream through my windows.

Crab Cakes

We never got there any later than seven a.m. Aunt Judy said if we did that our spot—which was the perfect spot—would be gone.

She would wake me at around six and we would take off from Tampa, over the causeway, to Clearwater Beach, which was a long and sandy strip of shell-strewn beach sprinkled with grills and picnic areas. There was a spot along the beach with the best water and breezes and tables and grills, and that spot was ours to claim on many summer mornings.

By the time we arrived, warm, caressing breezes and cool, lapping waves already were at work. Together they balanced the temperature equation.

My aunt and I would wade out a few feet from shore and hammer poles into the water's bed. Attached to each pole was a length of twine to which we had tied a raw chicken neck. Leaving poles and lines to lure our catch, we would return to our spot, set up chairs, stack towels and lay out blankets. Then Aunt Judy would bring out the bushel basket and make sure the lid fit securely while I got the short-handled nets. We were ready.

By now it would be close to nine, and we would play cards and keep an eye on our lines while waiting for the others to arrive. The lines would tell us when it was time. When they drew taut we would grab a net and slowly enter the water. We would take a line and gently draw it closer, and closer. Suddenly we could see our catch. At just the right moment we would pull up the line and scoop the net under a real beauty of a crab. Then we'd throw the line back out and endeavor to deposit the crab into the basket. This could be tricky. The crabs and their pincers scored many points against us and our fingers. But we usually managed to get sixty to a hundred by day's end.

At around eleven, my uncle would arrive with my two cousins, inner tube floats, food and Susie the dog who barked at crabs and waves and wind.

We three girls would run into the water and float while the sun beat down and the waves bobbed us along.

Soon the smell of barbecue would fill the air, and our mouths would water. My uncle was from Alabama. His sauce was the nectar of the South. We would fill ourselves with meat sandwiches dripping with sauce, corn cooked on the grill and salad. We'd top that off with cold, sweet watermelon that would drip down our arms as we ate.

We'd spend the thirty minutes that we had to wait before going back into the water by building sand castles with great paper-cup towers and dug-out moats. Once back in the water we would bob and laugh until it was time to go.

By five we were back home, showered and as red as our new-boiled crabs. We would all sit around and pick the meat from the shells and try not to get caught eating as we picked. Aunt Judy used the meat for crab salad and the best deviled crab cakes in the world.

I can close my eyes and taste those crab cakes or feel the waves or the warmth and smell the salt of the sea.

When Duluth's winter begins and then lingers on, windy and cold and gray, it's nice to know that there's a place in your heart and your memory that you can visit at a moment's notice, especially when that place is the perfect spot.

Savory Summer

❧

*I*just read in a magazine that the summer months are high stress and anxiety months. Obviously that survey was not done locally, where every moment outside brings a potpourri of delights for the senses. It is simply a "feel good about life" time.

If I were powerful enough to dictate how a perfect season should be, I couldn't do any better than a classic Duluth summer. Now in case it's a jinx to put that in print, remember that you didn't read it here. But it goes like this:

Showers arrive in the late afternoon and last just long enough to gently cool the evening breezes. Thunderstorms must come late at night when you can put your head under the covers and wonder why, ever since you were little, you always felt safer there. You also have time to remember the scientific reasons why thunder isn't scary.

And the people are everywhere. Freed from the bondage of heavy clothing, snow, ice and cold, they are walking and running, skating and playing.

In addition, all of us, in our own way, enjoy the hundred-carat sapphire that lies at our feet in the form of Lake Superior.

I will sit and watch a sailboat glide over the water as if being pulled by an imaginary string. I will watch a family on a boating outing, guys on a fishing trip, or a lithe young person water-skiing. It's all simply beautiful. And it's easy to be happy that they are happy. Somehow you share their joy vicariously because the lake is a unique bond that we share.

In this perfect time (which, remember, I never mentioned) everything is lush. As far as the eye can see there is green. Clumps of trees are so dense with foliage that you feel as though you are Goldilocks wandering too deep into the woods even though you are in your own neighborhood.

Certainly not an "also ran" for honors of the season is the color—apple blossoms, tulips, lilacs and geraniums in great arrays of white, pink, purple and red. Then there are the multitudes of beautiful plants with wonderful blooms and horrible botanical names like *Argeonemous Bisectus.* Science is fine, but heaven knows we all call it the bushy dark green plant with the tiny yellow buds.

Yet there is nothing more perfect about summer than the smells. They have a way of taking you to some other place and some other time. The summer's produce, with its sweet aromatic mixture of nectarine, peach and strawberry, transports me back home, where I can feel the sun on my face and cool dirt under my bare feet as I walk the rows in the picking fields. I must be ten and I want every berry and tomato that I see. Later that night I also remember suffering the distress of the "One-fer Syndrome." That's caused by little hands that go "one fer the bucket and one fer me."

The odor of suntan lotion equates to the beach. I can hear waves crashing, and I feel the crunchy sand. Then there is the sticky feeling that salt water leaves on your skin, coupled with the memory of my sister's hands in mine as we bob up and over the waves of the ocean.

The beach also means deli goodies. Mama would pack cold meat sandwiches and us and head to the water. To this day, salami without sand just isn't complete.

You can't conjure up the smells of the season

without mentioning the hickory and smoke that wafts over the back yards as we all rediscover fire and barbecue. Dozens of neighbors and party-goers and, in our case, baseball teams, are fed an indeterminable number of burgers and brats over that old Weber.

So let the magazines write about summer stress and anxiety as we languish in the sun, enjoy the water, take in the beauty and savor the sights, smells and tastes that we cherish. We who share this little bit of heaven are chomping berries, tossing food on the grill and enjoying the north country's perfect summer. But remember: you didn't read it here.

Treasures

As I write this I am at what is known as the Gopher Classic, a premier American Legion baseball tournament in the Twin Cities that draws teams from Las Vegas to Duluth. Major league and college scouts are all over the place.

The tournament is fun and provides some memorable baseball thrills. It is also the time I had planned to fully enjoy some warm weather, as Duluth has had mostly scattered summer to this point.

I packed my lightweight shirts, my bug spray and my suntan lotion. By the second day of the tournament, I was shopping for a sweatshirt, scrounging for an umbrella and shaking out a musty blanket from the trunk of the car. I was feeling unloved by Mother Nature.

This morning, though, on Day Three, I awoke to sunny skies and warm breezes. I am happy and totally forgiving of every rotten day previous to this one.

I also have suddenly realized how every day I become more and more a Northlander, one of those amazing people who are so grateful for one glorious day that it can make them forget months of cold, wind, ice and snow. It is now that we become like a butterfly and break out of our cocoons to be active and enjoy the outdoors.

After a winter of snow, I see bicycles on the sidewalk and I can be age six with my uncle yelling, "Keep pedaling!" as he lets me go and I ride alone, enjoying a child's first taste of freedom.

I hear the ping … ponk … ping … ponk of tennis ball and racket. The boys are little again and we all play tennis together.

One sound leads to another and I hear water gently lapping the shoreline of the warmth of the Atlantic Ocean. The sand is so hot. I'm with my sister and mother.

We spread out the blanket, secure it against the breeze with shoes on the corners and laugh as Mama takes off her glasses and we have to lead her to the water. I can feel the bobbing motion as the three of us play "ride the waves." We are so proud to be fearless as we hold onto Mama for dear life.

I get a whiff of a barbecue and I am with our dearest friends, who are now in Georgia.

That memory takes me to the Fourth of July. We barbecue up a storm. We swim and play Whiffle Ball during the day. The men play football and we watch fireworks. Then, while children sleep or occupy themselves, we adults play cards.

I miss that day so very much and have learned to treasure the sights and smells that bring the memories back to me.

Popping corn and steaming hot dogs; chattering and laughing. Memories somewhere deep inside that can be rekindled by a warm breeze or happy sound or familiar smell.

Memories of a moment of total freedom when we first ran with the wind or biked down a hill or rode the waves. The memories are warm and they comfort me.

Dream Game

I sat on the bleachers at the Ordean baseball field, and to any onlooker I was alone. In a backroom at the stadium, a bevy of men was waiting for scores from other fields so they could determine the seedings for the championship round of the Lakeview baseball tournament.

Meanwhile, there I was staring at what appeared to be a field that was finished for that day and readied for the next. The grass was shading toward emerald, the dirt was rich and smooth. A tarp was stretched across the home plate area and over the pitcher's mound to protect them. A cool breeze was blowing under a clear sky, and I felt as though I was at total peace.

Only moments earlier on that field had been vigorous young men—summer gladiators—whose weapons were aluminum bats and whose enemy was a small, hard ball.

Only moments earlier coaches had been signaling instructions. Fans had been bolstering egos with shouts of "good eye!" or "good swing!" and had cheered and chatted and "oohed" and "aahed" and loved the team and hated the ump and made the game a social outing, too.

Moments earlier you could smell the freshly made popcorn as its aroma wafted through the air as seductive as any temptress. Refreshment stands provided a bounty of fresh hot coffee and icy cool pop and the incomparable taste treat known as the ballpark hotdog.

Ostensibly, however, that was all over now. The popcorn machine was turned off and cleaned out. The coffeepot was washed and turned upside down, and I sat on the bleachers alone. It was then I realized that a ballfield never closes down.

As I sat there, I saw my boy Steve. He died in 1987, but on this day there he was on the mound, and he was pitching a good game. With every pitch his cap fell off and he stooped to pick it up and put it back on.

His teammates really wanted him to do well and they cheered for his successful pitches. I watched him play for his high school, VFW and

Legion teams—a dozen games in a few seconds—
and I saw him clearly as I had seen the young men
on the Ordean field only moments before.

I sat transfixed as Gary played third base for
his high school team, again in my memory. It was
his happiest time because he felt so sure of his play
and himself. He was at the plate and he was hit-
ting with power as he could do so well.

Gary has hung up his cleats now and doesn't
play ball. But he had his moments, and they lived
again on that day at Ordean as I watched homers
and great plays and victories and defeats. Ordean
was my theater and my memory was the film.

Suddenly, back in real time, a group of young
men from a Roseville team came to see the field.
They were impressed, and then one young man
saw me staring at the field. He said to a teammate,
"Looks like that lady is at her own Field of
Dreams."

I wanted to invite him to watch with me—
not one game, but dozens of them. I wanted to
share the smell of the popcorn, the cheers of the
crowd and the joy of Steve and Jimmy, also gone,
and the Dannys and Garys and Ericks and Todds
who armed themselves, faced the enemy and created the moments that keep this field and all fields
forever alive with boys and baseball.

Cry from
the Soul

Several days after our boy Steven was buried, someone put a baseball on the middle of his grave. When we saw it we cried shamelessly because a person unknown to us was sharing our pain.

A few weeks later, I was visiting the gravesite and saw that the baseball had been stolen. Pure, meaningless vandalism had robbed us of something precious, and the wail in me began from the very depth of my soul.

Far away, in another state, the grave of Ryan White, the young boy who died of AIDS, has been grossly vandalized three times. I've seen a picture of his mother at her child's grave. There was such agony in her face that I wanted to hold her hand as she reached for the wail that would come from the very depth of her soul.

While the desecration in our case was pointless, the violations against the Whites were willful and malicious. Mrs. White continues to work for public education about the AIDS virus; hate-mongers turn her efforts against her to persecute her and Ryan, whose personal battle has ended although he cannot yet rest. Hate exists all the time and is out there like a savage, ready to strike without warning.

Hatred is an umbrella that does not protect; instead, spokes of bias, bigotry, fear, misconception and ignorance radiate under its dark canopy.

I have been hate's victim and I know it strikes like a viper and it hurts. Here in Duluth I have heard many say, "You know I'm not a bigot, so I know you won't be hurt …" and then proceed to say something derogatory about my Jewish faith.

As a woman, I earned degrees and honors. In the seventies I was promised jobs but then not given them because they were managerial and no one wanted to train someone in her childbearing years.

I have heard women athletes being put down

and women's athletics described as boring and slow moving.

As a fat person, I have had to live with the stereotype that we are slovenly, lazy and stupid.

There is job discrimination and public discrimination.

My husband bought me a health club membership at the Y. When I went to see it, I was so scoffed at that I never returned. It is hard to become the ideal if you are expected to be the ideal going in.

Social circles are also discriminatory but are more subtle.

I would hope, however, that no one would be so biased against me for any of these things that they would kill me, and yet indeed they could. We have a new crime in the nineties: Hate Murder. And it comes so easy to our society because it radiates from the umbrella: I don't understand you; I fear you; you are different; I hate you; I kill you!

A young man in the Cities was a victim of hate murder. I don't know if he was Jewish or fat, but I do know he was said to be homosexual. Hate struck him down without warning.

In the aftermath of his death, everyone seemed to have an opinion regarding murdering someone for being a homosexual. But the debate is a false screen, and we need to remove the protective glass and look into the fire because murder is not the issue. The issue is the continuance of hatred and all that it entails in ourselves and our children.

Hatred lives in the form of a large Neo-Nazi movement in this country. Hatred thrives in the form of the Klu Klux Klan that is growing across the nation.

How involved are any of us in this silent killer that is spreading and destroying ideals as it makes its way into towns and cities?

It is too great an issue for me to bemoan the death of one man or to accept the label Hate Murder. I feel I should still be mourning the witches who died at Salem and the millions who died at the whim of Hitler and all who have been brutalized by the Klan.

But, for all who have suffered hate, I will symbolically hold the hand of Ryan White's mother and wail, from the very depth of my soul.

Tick ... Tick

As my sister and I got older and our lives blended, we shared many crazy moments. We can still talk pig latin as fast as we can speak English. We both remember the day when I swam beneath her to give her the confidence she needed to pass a pool lap test.

I taught her to dance, and she gave me the joy of holding a baby niece. We fought and we made up, and together we can laugh harder and enjoy more than any two people I know.

From the day she became twenty-one I have called her "old hag" on her birthday, and this year I sent her a banner with the sentiment.

Now she is fifty. When did it happen, this time thing?

Thinker

For the second half of my life I will be a philosopher. I will have great thoughts and propose ageless questions upon which generations can ponder.

Because of my philosopher's role, when I am thinking I will actually be working.

I'm not sure how the mechanics will work. For example, do I hang a shingle: The Philosopher Is In? Would it be better if I walked the sidewalks with a sign: Will Think For Food?

Obviously this is not an easy field to break into. Also, what gimmick can I use to attract clientele?

Maybe I could have a business card that

promises: "I will bear the burden of your weighty issues."

I wonder what philosophy majors really do (see—I'm born for this occupation). If they don't teach, then where are they and what are they doing? Are there any modern-day great thinkers? The last one I remember was Dobie Gillis. He sat under the statue of Rodin and pondered questions of life and love.

Delving into this topic is like opening Pandora's Box. We all think, but who judges thoughts? What makes one person a mediocre thinker and another a great thinker? We all know that to attain greatness, one needs to practice, and yet people who spend hours sitting and thinking tend to be labeled bums. We need to be more careful lest we discourage a Twenty-First Century philosopher in the making.

Deep thinking is nothing new to the Scherer household. I can remember the kids arguing over which came first—the chicken or the egg.

What are today's unsolvable and timeless questions? There will always be, "Who am I?" but that isn't universal like this Scherer family favorite: If a tree crashes down in the woods and no one is there to hear it, does it make a noise? That is a priceless question and doesn't cause bad feelings like, "Is there a God?"

But where are the new queries? Who will propose the questions for tomorrow's family of philosophical thinkers? Answer: I will!

I can see it has to be me. First, I care. Second, I noticed the need. And, third, I have the time to think, even if only after the tax season.

I know this burning issue is eased by the fact that I have proclaimed myself the Messiah of Solveless Thought, but I want people to understand that I am not just jumping into the arena unprepared. I believe I have a question worthy of empty, yet deep, discussion.

And, because you are my following, I will allow you to wrestle with this issue. (I'm nervous about going into print, but Plato and Socrates can't hold onto their dual greatness forever!)

So, here it is, my first great thought: When I'm engaged in the long, hard hours of tax preparation, am I working in the still of the night, or am I working in the wee small hours of the morning?

Is midnight the still of the night and one, two and three o'clock the wee, small hours? Or are one, two and three the still of the night and 3:01 to 6:00 a.m. the wee, small hours?

Face it, this is as good as the tree in the forest question, and I've only just begun.

Rest easy. I'm out there—and I'm thinking for you!

Irreconcilable Food Groups

D ivorce is a sad and ugly truth. And while it is all too frequent, I am a proponent of two unhappy people separating to become two happy people, one hopes, when all else has failed.

While I accept the concept, though, I still wonder about one of the oft-cited reasons for divorce.

I can understand divorce because of adultery, abuse of any kind, neglect, communication blockades and even changing lifestyles and growing apart, but I have a real problem with "irreconcilable differences."

It is my humble opinion that the very institution of marriage—two strangers deciding to live as a unit—is a breeding ground for irreconcilable differences.

I have been married for twenty-six years. I knew going into this union that my husband was a Northern Protestant Republican, while I was a Southern Jewish Democrat. I haven't been surprised by the big differences. But over the years, sneaky, subtle differences have surfaced, and they exist in every area of our life together.

Alan believes in a wholistic approach to healing. He buys dozens of pamphlets and magazines that promise to contain some little known health secret. "Flush pain with papaya" or "Rid yourself of headaches with oregano" are only two of a hundred examples.

I, on the other hand, tackle pain with two aspirin and a call to my doctor in the morning. The only concession to Alan's viewpoint is taking the aspirin with the papaya juice he had bought in preparation for his big flush.

It took time for me to discover that my mate is a middle-outer while I'm an edges-inner. To my husband, a plate of food is to be dug into and enjoyed. As I eat, on the other hand, I keep pushing my various food groups to the middle until they're all gone.

Alan takes a handful of popcorn and seems totally unconcerned that some makes it to his mouth while some settles on someplace rather than in his stomach. I eat popcorn a kernel or two at a time. I will even lick my finger and bunch up poppy seeds if they drop off a roll.

I sleep straight. I go to sleep on my right side and then, to ensure even wear, I turn to my left side sometime in the night.

I married the Happy Wanderer. He starts in the middle, straight as an arrow, and ends up on a diagonal with his trunk in the middle and his legs across to my side. This leaves me in a fetal position, desperately clinging to a quarter of my half of the bed.

Then there's the really big issue … toilet paper. No matter how often I explain and complain, if Alan goes shopping he buys white toilet paper. My bathroom is black and pink, so obviously white doesn't work! Solid pink is an acceptable second, but the room cries out for a pink floral print. Am I the only one to whom this makes perfect sense, the only one who realizes the sublime wisdom of my decoration scheme?

Television watching is another area of discussion. I must watch a show from the very first minute or I couldn't care less. Alan can come in after an hour, become totally engrossed and then utter the infamous three little words: "Fill me in." How? There are sixteen characters, three affairs, illegitimate children, two murders and a good guy.

"Have you seen my (fill in the blank): glasses/comb/wallet/checkbook/car keys?" He misplaces things. I don't.

And he saves everything. I don't.

And he loves me even though he could easily write an article about his nutty wife who insists that white toilet paper doesn't work and even wets her finger to peck at poppy seeds. It's probably enough to drive him crazy.

In any event, it's a twenty-six-year-old love affair plainly wrought with irreconcilable differences.

Home Alone

*A*lan had gone to see his mother in New Jersey and to take care of business for her there. He would be gone for four days. I had time to myself.

I was more than a little apprehensive about his leaving, especially because it was winter. Every time Alan steps onto a plane and leaves, the weather sets out to get me. In his absence over the years we have had snowstorms and icestorms and flooding, all of which render me unable to drive —or walk, for that matter—because I still abide by Miami-based rules for when I may venture out. But, like it or not, Alan would be gone, and I would have time to myself.

Day One would be devoted to housecleaning. If I was going to settle in warm and cozy, then the surroundings had to be clean.

I was free to do as I pleased. However, at around six-thirty—because we always eat at around six-thirty, I guess—I fixed a chicken breast and salad and ate leisurely. A quick cleanup put me in front of the TV, settled in, and, within minutes, fast asleep. No problem with Day One and time to myself.

On Day Two I awoke around eight and read the paper without having to share it. This was the best part of my alone experience. Each section was in order, and I didn't have to turn any section back to the beginning or wrestle with any pages put back messily.

After the perfect-paper afterglow, I was faced with a whole Friday. My house was clean, and I didn't have to cook, so I could get some bigger projects done.

I decorated the Christmas tree and finished setting up my tax office. Around two in the afternoon I decided to have some entertainment and rented two movies, Beauty and the Beast and Sister Act. I didn't want anything heavy or emotional, just some entertaining fluff during this time to myself. When Alan called, I was crying after watching Beauty and the Beast. You can't even trust Disney anymore.

Dinner alone came around six-thirty again and consisted of a burger patty and salad. Later I settled in front of the TV and, before falling asleep, reflected on my time to myself. I had read and completed two projects and relaxed and gotten some work done. Now, at the end of Day Two, I felt I should reach out a little. Day Three would be a bit more stimulating.

Saturday and I were ready. I made a few calls, but found all my friends either with their families or doing household chores. I called the boys and got their answering machines. So good to hear their voices and the instruction to leave a message at the sound of the beep. This was not good. I was going for hours without speaking.

I could have gone shopping, but I hate purposeful shopping, much less aimless shopping. Besides, it was snowing. The weatherman called it unpredicted. Why hadn't he called me? I could have predicted it, what with Alan gone.

My biggest problem, though, was that I was talking back to the people on TV. They would say something and I would make nasty remarks back to them.

At dinnertime (six-thirty again), I called for Chinese home delivery. After that I settled in front of the TV once more, and in desperation turned on the shopping network. This was great! All the hosts were talking, and it was as though they were talking to me. People called them, and I heard their conversations. I listened for several hours and it didn't bother me that I was being treated like an idiot. After all, I could talk back to them as I had to the others on TV, but these people were my friends. And it could have been true that the Budweiser beer can slippers they were selling would make me more popular.

And then it was Day Four and Alan would return. I had had time to myself, enough time to realize that such moments are deeply personal. The need for time to myself is an occasional twenty-four- to thirty-six-hour need, and then I'm enough in touch with my yin and yang to know that life at its best is life shared.

Mega Prep

When we moved from Miami to Duluth back in 1981, my first impulse was to stock up for those future times when, due to the weather, we would be trapped like animals and unable to connect with other life forms.

Before I had the chance to do that, however, a friend told me to forget it. She had come from New Mexico many years before with the same thought and, with no one to stop her, had acted upon that fear. Years later, however, she had thrown out very old powdered milk and canned goods.

Over the next ten years, I found her advice

to be sound. I learned that storms don't stop Duluth. And besides, I'm not sure that I could ever bring myself to use a ten-year-old can of anything.

Today, though, my pantry holds items that are in great number, and you will understand the reason for this now that I can finally reveal my own personal saga of the Halloween Megastorm.

As in any story, first the stage must be set. I need to explain my provisions cycle. I grocery shop on Saturday or Sunday for meals I have planned through Thursday. This cycle evolved, like most things in my life, because of the boys' sports. Friday was often a football game or a baseball tournament night. Many times we were away, or life was just not conducive to sit-down dinners.

Further, I'm not one who stockpiles the freezer, as I often need its space for catering. My pantry has always been depleted by the boys anyway, and I restock only when they are coming home.

The purpose here is for you to get a clear picture that by most Fridays, Mother Hubbard and I are soul sisters.

It is now two p.m. on Storm Friday and I hear a faint, "Help me!" I go to the door and see a six- or seven-foot drift, which has my husband in it. I am able to inch the door open and pull him out, which, in turn, enables him to squeeze into the house. He has come home in someone's truck. His car is at work downtown. We cozy through the afternoon and playfully scrounge for dinner.

Saturday morning Alan is ready to take on Mother Nature and all her wrath. He edges out of the house and attacks what is now an even larger drift. He is halfway down the walk when his disc slips. I bed him down and baby him and garner all my inner strength to get us through. We lunch on deli from the refrigerator that I am never sure of even after smelling it.

It is now that I realize the awful truth: "You'll always be okay" is a myth. We are about to run out of toilet paper.

And, to make matters worse, we are already using sleeves for tissues, hand towels for napkins and a sponge in lieu of paper towels. We are paper-product-less.

I run downstairs to check my party supply drawer and find six Styrofoam balls and little gold ashtrays. I forage on my hands and knees and find two red napkins in the pantry that were left from Joey's graduation party. What, I wonder, would Laura Ingalls Wilder do?

What would anyone do? Yes, but you have to

separate the sections to get a really nice shred of the newspaper.

That night for dinner we have rice and canned tomatoes and for an air of festivity I serve it with two red napkins.

Sunday morning we enjoy black coffee with crackers and good or possibly bad cheese nestled on shredded paper. My street isn't plowed and wouldn't be until noon.

The walk isn't shoveled and our car is still downtown. The driveway people we called will plow us out the next day for sure, they say. That happens eight days and four companies later.

The taxi we call will be there in an hour. We cancel after two and a half hours. Then a friend comes and takes Alan to his car. By now, my inner strength has faded and I am feeling abandoned and removed from all life forms that aren't radio disc jockeys.

We go to the store and I buy steak and Pepsi and lots of paper products. But I shop only through Tuesday. After all, I have to get back in cycle and don't want to stock up too much.

However, my pantry does now contain forty-eight rolls of toilet paper. After all, it can't go bad.

Instant
Gratification

I am in the middle of a nightmare, and, as hard as I try, I see no escape. It all started innocently enough: A large brown envelope arrived in the mail. Knowing what it was, I tossed it on the kitchen table. My son later glanced at the mail and commented on the promised riches of cars, homes, vacations and money that this envelope held. I scoffed at the whole idea, but later that evening, when seated at the table, I opened Pandora's Box. Inside was The American Dream: Get Rich Quick … Never Worry … Possess ALL YOU EVER WANTED!!!

I was helpless. How could I deprive my loved ones of all they ever wanted?

The next words I read sealed my fate: "Last year's winner didn't enter and threw away all these riches." (I know now that this person actually had entered in previous years and later asked the government for a new identity to avoid this kind of mail ... but I jump ahead.)

Once opened, the envelope revealed a wealth of brochures, a sheet of stamps, an entry form and various smaller coupons that merely had to be signed so I could win a VCR, microwave or big-screen TV. To win the car I had to find two car stamp halves and pick the color I wanted. The dream vacation stamp went on the outside of the reply envelope, but collecting the ten million dollars, well, that required finding stamps and ordering or not ordering magazines. I ordered two regarding food preparation. I do some catering in the months after the tax season. What a deal! I would win all these riches—and do it with a tax write-off!

After checking the checklist for entrants I realized that because I ordered magazines I could have used the express entry and been automatically entered in everything. I still wonder, if I had done that, how they would have known I wanted my Cadillac to be silver.

I mailed the small brown reply envelope—and it miraculously heeded that Biblical admonition: "Become fruitful and multiply."

Within days I was besieged by new sweep-stakes. I got more brown envelopes, and then came the flood of official notifications. These were emblazoned with official seals and declared me a sure winner. The notifications were only the forerunners.

Later came a catalog along with the assurance that I had won anywhere from two dollars to a hundred thousand dollars. These are pre-selected numbers and my fate was already cast, but to find out exactly where I was on this chain of chance I had to send the numbers back ... and perhaps order something at the same time.

While all this was going on I was still under fire from the various magazine contests. I was advancing levels and had to re-enter and re-enter— and now there were deadlines. I knew the winners weren't lucky at all; they were even more obsessed than the system. Each entry was taking me close to a half-hour of locating car halves and color choices and vacation spots and making decisions such as how I wanted the money paid to me. Alan and I almost fought about it.

Just as I had the system beat, the phone calls started. I got one from Rick, one from Carol and one from Jeff. I had somehow become a President's Club member, and they were calling to offer me TWENTY-SIX MAGAZINES for which they would pay the first sixty months.

THAT'S FIVE YEARS! I would need an addition to my home.

The envelopes kept coming. By now I was a true finalist, a semi-finalist, a quarter-finalist and a final finalist. In truth I have no idea how many or what contests I have entered. Every day, when the mail comes, I pray I haven't inadvertently ordered a camel.

As for the American dream, I quizzed my family to see what their fantasy possessions were. After new cars, Alan would like some new clothes; Gary wants compact discs; Joe would add to his already-large collection of baseball caps; and I would like the contraption that slides between your stove and counter so dirt and food don't drop down there.

In all fairness, I should let you know that last week I did receive winnings. I won't tell which figure I won, but I will say that it cost me a dollar and sixty-five cents to win it because I had to re-enter four times and that left me unable to round my winnings to a dollar. When I had won, Alan could see the tension drain from my face.

And then it happened ... the nightmare revisited ... the sequel! Because I wasn't a big winner, but was so valued to them, the sweepstakes sponsors of their own accord entered me in their second-chance contest. I should be getting my envelope any day now.

Putting it Together

For most people, the tax season just comes and goes. Except for some media hype regarding last-minute filers, April 15 is just another day.

But for me, it is much more.

I earn a second family income, as so many others do, but I do it basically in sixteen weeks.

That demands that I use as many of the allotted twenty-four hours of the day and seven days of the week as I can. After twenty-plus years in the tax business I am programmed to produce the adrenalin that is required to work days that begin at four a.m. and end at midnight. When people ask me how I do it, I admit that I'm not sure. Toward the end of the season, I begin to plan for my post-season "to-do's." I think that keeps me going.

This year, for example, I'm going to clean out my closet. After nine years of accumulating, it's goodbye to all the larger clothes from when I gained weight and all the smaller clothes from when I lost weight and the clothes that never fit at any weight.

I am going to straighten out my dresser drawers. I have scarves too wrinkled to wear; gloves from my prom; pins, buttons, and souvenirs from every function I ever attended; and lingerie. The lingerie is of two types: Barbie doll size and the "heaven forbid you should be wearing these and have an accident and go to the hospital and be seen in them" kind. Goodbye to that mess!

I am going to throw out the "needs mending" pile. It's so old that no one recognizes the clothes anymore.

My bathroom has a closet with six shelves. The closet was built, I am sure, with towels in mind. Now it has room for everything except towels. They have to be stuffed in and around the other "vital" junk in there. Goodbye to that clutter! I'm going to arrange the closet alphabetically, if need be.

And there are the pillow covers I was crocheting for my son's dorm room when he went off to college. He is near the end of his freshman year, and I'm determined to finish those covers … though they would make a nice wedding gift. Yessir, and I'm going to have a garage sale.

I have been putting things away for years and labeling them "Garage Sale Stuff!" My family has always asked, "What garage sale?" Well, here it is— time for the big one. Goodbye, Garage Sale Stuff!

Then the drapes need to be cleaned, the curtains washed, and I'm going to scrub the kitchen cabinets. It's time to decorate the downstairs and wallpaper my bedroom. I'm going to read anything I want to—for pleasure, not business—and watch sit-coms and talk shows.

The list is endless.

There is so much, and I have fantasized about all of these "to-do's" for weeks, knowing that soon this day would come—the day when I could say, "It's over for another year!"

I owe myself one really nice day of rest and then I'll not be rushed and I'll have time and … you know … I really haven't a clue what I'll do.

Actually, after all these years, I do know that after the tax season I need time to reflect. Have you ever been so harried and fragmented by life's demands that you had no time to think? I need to be the king's men and put Humpty-Dumpty back together again.

I don't know why, but I have always felt that the movement of water is saying something about life. It fascinates me.

So I will spend some time along the shores of Lake Superior. I will watch the water come in slowly and gain momentum, like a happening in one's life.

I will watch it crash onto the rocks and shore with great force, and I will think of the things that have had a crashing effect on my life … things that are vital only today, and things that are always there.

The water will spray into droplets and be the many roles we all play in life, and then the water will come together again and peacefully be drawn back to become part of the whole again—the lake at peace.

I will have gone to the shore a mass of puzzle pieces … I will have reflected … I will have laughed and cried and let the movement of the water tell me its story of life, and when I have left, I too will be whole again.

When Lilacs Bloom

༭

I might have been immune to the beauty of plants and flowers. After all, I grew up in the sub-tropics of South Florida, where color is everywhere. South Florida *is* beautiful, but it is always beautiful—which is probably why I was never enthralled by it all.

Since moving to Duluth, however, my appreciation level for natural beauty has skyrocketed. Because I didn't have seasonal changes when I was growing up, I am awestruck now by the annual progression from subdued blue-green pine and white snow to so much green in all shades and explosions of color everywhere.

I know there is a seemingly endless period of

rain and slush between the beautiful seasons of winter and summer. But we seem to be able to accept the slushy period because when it is over the trees suddenly are full and tulips looking like daubs of color from an artist's brush are standing proud. Geraniums in their red, white and pinkness are at every turn, and the magnificence of the flowering crab is breathtaking. You walk or drive, and every view is better than the one before. It is wonderful!

However, even when I first saw this "busting out all over," the flowers that overwhelmed me were the lilacs. I had never seen them before, and I fell deeply in love.

I would drive around to places where I knew they were growing in great numbers so I could savor their beauty and smell. To my amazement and disappointment, I learned that they bloom for only a short time. How, I wondered, could we be given something so utterly perfect to have it fill our lives for only a short period of time?

When the lilacs were gone I wanted them back so badly. I was almost blinded to the fact that to enjoy them I had to accept the shortness of their stay with us and focus instead on the total joy they gave us while they bloomed.

This love affair with the lilac became very personal. I had to have one.

Outside my kitchen door was a low-growing

fir of some sort. I have seen some firs that are lovely, but this one wasn't. It grew with a flat middle and bushy, out of control sides—like your hair in the morning after a restless night.

Three years after we came to Duluth I bought two small lilac trees and announced that the homely fir was history and that the spot right outside my kitchen door would be the new home for these lilacs.

My oldest son, Steven, took on the formidable task of planting. He used shovel and pick and a saw and worked so hard to dig up that fir. He spoke of its root structure quite explicitly. I can still see him, shirtless and in shorts, working with such vigor that the muscles of his arms and back stood out and he glistened with the sweat of his labor. I took him lemonade, and he laughed at the flowerless twigs he was laboring to plant.

Several days later I got up and was urged by a Cheshire cat-grinning Steven to go outside. There were my twigs, full of lilacs. He had gotten up at four-thirty a.m. and, before going out on his paper route, had clipped lilacs from around the neighborhood and taped them to my bushes. We laughed. But we usually laughed.

Steven was a brilliant honor student with great wit and quiet charm. Being with him made you feel good. He adored his family and was a good friend. He also loved sports and was known to set his alarm for some unearthly hour to watch water polo on TV.

We have a letter written to us that describes him as "suntanned with soft hair and a Tom Cruise smile." The letter goes on to say that Steven thought guys who treated women poorly were jerks and that he always had good advice and time for everyone who needed him.

Steven was totally unaware of how special he was, and this only added to his appeal. He was at the University of Minnesota studying for an exam before he was to be off to New Orleans for Spring Break when at the age of nineteen he died. The cause of death remains unknown.

He was not perfect. He could be lazy, he made procrastination an art form and he loved to tease his younger brothers mercilessly. However, following his death we received testimonials from teachers, friends and others. During a memorial service that the students at the university gave him, they spoke of him spontaneously for two and a half hours.

It makes you wonder why we are given something so utterly perfect to have it for only a moment in time. Yet, when I open my kitchen door and see my two big lilac trees full to capacity with blooms, I put aside that thought and instead focus on the joy Steven gave us while he lived.